❦❦❦

MEETING
THE
CHALLENGES
OF CHANGE

❦❦❦

When Life Comes
Apart at the Seams

❦❦❦

Devotional Daybooks
By Neva Coyle

Making Sense of Pain and Struggle
Meeting the Challenges of Change
A New Heart . . . A New Start

A Devotional Daybook

by Neva Coyle

❤❤❤

MEETING THE CHALLENGES OF CHANGE

❤❤❤

When Life Comes
Apart at the Seams

❤❤❤

BETHANY HOUSE PUBLISHERS
MINNEAPOLIS, MINNESOTA 55438

Copyright © 1993
Neva Coyle
All Rights Reserved

Published by Bethany House Publishers
A Ministry of Bethany Fellowship, Inc.
6820 Auto Club Road, Minneapolis, Minnesota 55438

Printed in the United States of America

Library of Congress Cataloging-in-Publication Data

Coyle, Neva, 1943–
    Meeting the challenges of change / Neva Coyle.
        p.   cm. — (A Devotional daybook)

    1. Women—Prayer–books and devotions—English. 2. Change—Religious aspects—Christianity—Prayer–books and devotions—English. 3. Devotional calendars.
I. Title. II. Series: Coyle, Neva, 1943–   Devotional daybook.
BV4527.C69   1993
242'.643—dc20   92–40388
ISBN 1–55661–278–8   CIP

To Rhonda

NEVA COYLE is Founder of Overeaters Victorious and President of Neva Coyle Ministries. Presently she is the Coordinator of Departmental Ministries in her church. Her ministry is enhanced by her bestselling books, tapes, as well as by her being a gifted motivational speaker/teacher. Neva and her husband make their home in California.

She may be contacted at:

P.O. Box 2330
Orange, CA 92669

Preface

I STOOD BESIDE the bed of my aged grandmother watching her die. I observed her labored breathing and examined the porcelain skin stretched across her veined and wrinkled hand. Grandma's breathing grew more shallow with each breath until she simply did not draw another. At her death I cried, but not for Grandma. She knew and loved Jesus. I cried for *me*. I could not imagine life without her. I grieved the loss of her in my life, I had to adjust to the empty place she left when she passed on.

A few years later I stood beside my daughter's bed—not a death bed, but a birthing bed. I held my firstborn grandchild—a grandson. The season had changed. No longer the grand-daughter, I was the grand*mother*.

I have experienced other changes of season. Moving, making new friends, finding a new church. Seasons of restlessness, times of personal examination and reevaluation. I've seen dreams die, fresh ideas born. I've had seasons of tears as well as laughter.

We all experience the seasons—changes. Some changes come because of decisions we have made ourselves. New opportunities beckoned. Some have come because of personal crisis or tragedy.

For all the changes we go through, the biggest change occurs *after* a decision is made, after the crisis hits, as we adjust to the new and let go of the old. Changes in our lives work changes within us.

After the baby is born, we work at becoming a mother. After graduation, we work at becoming the dentist, the paralegal, the administrator we have studied so hard to be. Following the transfer to a new job, we work at familiarizing ourselves with the new company's policies and procedures. After accepting Jesus Christ, we begin to run the Christian race.

We can decide for change, or change can take us by surprise. Either way, if we don't prepare ourselves for the challenge that follows, we can become overwhelmed and falter. To face the challenge of transition, we need to know how to call on additional strength, wisdom, and inner resources. That's what this book is about—facing the challenge of change.

Contents

How to Use This Book

THIS DEVOTIONAL STUDY is designed to fit easily into a busy schedule. It is divided into six sections, with five entries in each section. If an entry is read each day, it will take just thirty days to complete the book. Take a few minutes each day to read the suggested Scripture reference and accompanying thoughts. The questions at the end of each entry will help you focus on a personal application of the Scripture selection.

If the book is used in a group study, members should study the five entries of a section during the week and then meet as a group to discuss the material. In this way the book will take six weeks to complete, or longer depending on the needs of the group. It is also easily adaptable to a ministry group that is already established or a Sunday school class.

If you are using this material in a group study, suggested guidelines and discussion questions are included at the end of the book for the use of the leader.

There is a time for everything,
  and a season for every activity under heaven:
a time to be born and a time to die,
a time to plant and a time to uproot,
a time to kill and a time to heal,
a time to tear down and a time to build,
a time to weep and a time to laugh
a time to mourn and a time to dance.
a time to scatter stones and a time to gather them,
a time to embrace and a time to refrain,
a time to search and a time to give up,
a time to keep and a time to throw away,
a time to tear and a time to mend,
a time to be silent and a time to speak,
a time to love and a time to hate,
a time for war and a time for peace.

ECCLESIASTES 3:1–8

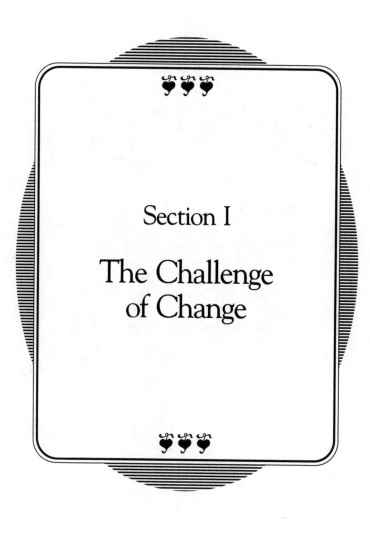

Section I

The Challenge
of Change

"WHEN, IN THE COURSE OF HUMAN EVENTS . . ."
The first line of the Declaration of Independence is familiar
to all American history students. I wonder if Thomas Jefferson
thought about his words as an apt description of every human
experience.

In the course of everyday human events, changes occur.
We may not welcome them, they may be hard, but changes
are inevitable.

As I write this book, I am facing changes. As you read
through these pages, you are facing changes. As we learn how
to handle change successfully, we grow and mature.

The first step in this growth is to acknowledge the inevi-
tability and even the difficulty of change. Digging our heels
in and denying the pain of transition can only wear down our
hope and, eventually, our faith.

With Christ as our Guide, we are not alone in a time of
transition. And yet getting from "here" to "there" takes time
and patience.

The changes you face now will be easier as you see them
in the larger context of life. What do changes in your life have
in common with mine or with the changes faced by biblical
characters who lived two thousand years ago? What challenge
does change present you with? In the first five chapters of this
study, we will consider these questions.

Chapter · 1 ·

The Challenge of Interruption

Meanwhile, Saul was still breathing out murderous threats against the Lord's disciples. He went to the high priest and asked him for letters to the synagogues in Damascus, so that if he found any there who belonged to the Way, whether men or women, he might take them as prisoners to Jerusalem. As he neared Damascus on his journey, suddenly a light from heaven flashed around him. He fell to the ground and heard a voice say to him, "Saul, Saul, why do you persecute me?"

"Who are you, Lord?" Saul asked.

"I am Jesus, whom you are persecuting," he replied. "Now get up and go into the city, and you will be told what you must do."

Acts 9:1–6

LATE IN AUGUST 1992, meteorologists noticed weather patterns over the Atlantic that could build into a tropical storm. A storm watch turned into a storm warning. Residents of south Florida were advised to prepare for Hurricane Andrew, which slammed onto shore in the middle of the night. Many evacuated their homes to wait out the storm's fury.

In community shelters or cowering in closets in their own

homes, they listened to the storm howling in rage. They could only guess at the devastation they would face when the storm abated. Andrew ripped apart entire communities. The storm whipped traffic signs as if they were children's toys, and shredded protective plywood into toothpicks. When the long night was finally over, and the winds had quieted, residents crept from their shelters to face the sight of total destruction—their homes, shopping centers, and schools were gone. Nothing would ever be the same again. The impact of one night of high winds would be felt in Homestead, Florida, for an entire generation.

———————

After his blinding, lightning-flash experience on the road to Damascus, I think Saul could have identified with Florida residents who survived Hurricane Andrew. Saul's conversion and the call of God on his life changed everything—even his identity. From that time on he was called Paul.

At some point in the course of our lives we all face change, and sometimes it means our life is changed forever. For Paul, the change was cause for joy and celebration—yet difficult. He was made literally blind for a time, and had to establish himself in a new community with a new circle of friends.

Acts 9, the story of Paul's personal Hurricane Andrew, begins with the simple word *meanwhile*.

One way to "get a handle on" even major change is to see it as an interruption. Life does not pause, allowing change to be put neatly into place.

In the "meanwhiles" of your life and mine, the storms of change may brew and strike—while we go about our daily routines, making everyday decisions about what to wear and what to eat.

Change interrupts routine. It may even throw us into chaos and turmoil. It can rearrange our life, challenge our beliefs, take possessions or even people from our lives, and we may not be ready or steady when the changes come.

Not every change will be devastating, like a Hurricane Andrew. Not every change will be remembered for the rest of your life. But every change will punctuate or interrupt the "meanwhiles"—as life goes on. Because *life* is change, and change is life.

But take comfort. The Lord of the universe knows your routine. And He also knows your interruptions. He wants to help you face and identify change as it comes.

What changes have you faced that changed the course of your life?

What changes—major or minor—are you facing now?

What routines have been interrupted?

Chapter · 2 ·

The Lure of the Familiar

> As Pharaoh approached, the Israelites looked up, and there were the Egyptians, marching after them. They were terrified and cried out to the LORD. They said to Moses, "Was it because there were no graves in Egypt that you brought us to the desert to die? What have you done to us by bringing us out of Egypt? Didn't we say to you in Egypt, 'Leave us alone; let us serve the Egyptians'? It would have been better for us to serve the Egyptians than to die in the desert!"
>
> Exodus 14:10–12

"DON'T CONFUSE ME with the facts. I've made up my mind." Have you heard someone quote that old cliché lately? For too many people it's not a joke. While they don't actually say the words, they live by them. How about you?

One of the greatest challenges of change is the confusion that follows—whether the change has been brought on by crisis or because of a well-thought-out decision.

Knowing and believing that "in all things God works for the good of those who love him" (Romans 8:28) does not necessarily prevent confusion. Think of it like this.

Your whole life is neatly—or maybe not so neatly—arranged like a closet. Something new needs to be added to that closet space, and this requires that everything previously stored be brought out so it can be reorganized and rearranged.

If you were to come to my house on a closet-cleaning day, you would see some confusion. Piles of items here and there make no sense to anyone—or so it would seem. But in the middle of all the confusion and disorder there is a plan. Some piles are "keepers," some are "tossers." But even when I have a plan in mind, I can feel temporarily overwhelmed. I might stop and wish I hadn't started the project. I just want things to be in order again, back the way they were.

That's how it is with change. Even with clear goals and noble purposes, we go through a stage when the new facts, friends, ideas, or environment threaten old cherished facts, ideas, etc. We find comfort in the familiar.

That's the way it was with God's people when they left Egypt. They didn't know how it was all going to turn out. They didn't know they would be free to head for the Promised Land after God had washed Pharaoh's chariots away in the Red Sea. They hadn't heard the outcome of the Bible story, or seen the Hollywood version. Faced with an impossible situation, they wanted to return to the way things used to be, even though that meant repressive slavery in a foreign land.

If God has led you into change and you suddenly feel confused, panicky, and eager to run back to the familiar, the comfort of the old ways—stop! Wait. Do not act rashly.

Give God time to give you more clear direction. Act on His truth and righteousness and His good plan, not on your fear of the unknown and the sometimes false "safety" you feel with the familiar.

The promise of Romans 8:28 will not keep you from confusion. But it will see you through it. Look around at the chaos and say to yourself: God is working through all of this for my good—because I love Him and I am called according to His purpose.

———

What familiar parts of your life has change robbed you of? List

22

ideas, people, places, things.

Write a prayer that expresses your confusion before God.

What new meaning does this verse have for you?
"Do not conform any longer to the pattern of this world, but be transformed by the renewing of your mind. Then you will be able to test and approve what God's will is—his good, pleasing and perfect will" (Romans 12:2).

The Challenge of Responsibility

Some time later, Jesus went up to Jerusalem for a feast of the Jews. Now there is in Jerusalem near the Sheep Gate a pool, which in Aramaic is called Bethesda and which is surrounded by five covered colonnades. Here a great number of disabled people used to lie—the blind, the lame, the paralyzed. One who was there had been an invalid for thirty-eight years. When Jesus saw him lying there and learned that he had been in this condition for a long time, he asked him, "Do you want to get well?"

"Sir," the invalid replied, "I have no one to help me into the pool when the water is stirred. While I am trying to get in, someone else goes down ahead of me."

Then Jesus said to him, "Get up! Pick up your mat and walk." At once the man was cured; he picked up his mat and walked.

John 5:1–9a

THIS WAS HIS moment! Jesus was standing right there, not to put the disabled man into the pool, but to eliminate the necessity for the pool! This man lived in hope of the moment when someone would help him so he could be healed. He'd waited for thirty-eight years, out of reach of the healing waters. Now, at this moment, even though the pool was still out of reach, wholeness was close at hand.

The man was in the right place at the right time, but Jesus asked a critical question: "Do you want to get well?" He had to decide what he really wanted.

Jesus knew the healing would not be complete until the man took some personal responsibility. He had to get up and walk. This took a step of genuine faith. In his infirmity he had relied on others. Now his responsibilities would increase.

What a transition took place for that man on this fateful afternoon! Not only was his body changed, his whole life was changed.

But at the instant of healing, Jesus didn't ask, "What are your goals? Where will you work? What will you do tomorrow?" He simply said, "Take up your bed and walk." In the morning the man was carried to the side of the pool; in the afternoon he was told to take up his bed and walk.

Didn't Jesus realize the tremendous adjustment the man would suffer after being helpless and dependent for so many years? Of course He did. But He also knew the importance of taking that first step of faith. Nothing would happen without that.

You see, responsibility doesn't come after you have made it safely through transition. Taking responsibility helps you make transition safely.

You have been asking Jesus to help you. You have been seeking wholeness. Now it is time to "take up your bed and walk." Are you willing?

———————

What responsibilities are you most tempted to let slide until "everything settles down"?

How has not taking responsibility hindered your time of transition?

How can taking responsibility help transition happen?

Chapter · 4 ·

The Challenge of Sorting

Finally, brothers, whatever is true, whatever is noble, whatever is right, whatever is pure, whatever is lovely, whatever is admirable—if anything is excellent or praiseworthy—think about such things. Whatever you have learned or received or heard from me, or seen in me—put it into practice. And the God of peace will be with you.

Philippians 4:8–9

IF WE APPROACH change with a positive outlook, we can expect our minds and spirits to be refreshed as they are released from outdated, "stiff" ideas that no longer fit. Think of those tight but great-looking shoes you've worn all evening. You're relieved to take them off when you get into your own home.

Now think back to the analogy of the closet-cleaning. There isn't room for everything—old and new—in that closet, unless I drastically rearrange and/or throw some things out. So everything comes out of the closet and is spread around the room in piles.

Right from the start I have to make decisions. There are two basic categories: "keep" and "toss." Actually, "toss" has two subcategories: "throw away" and "give away."

Eventually I concentrate on the "keepers"; sorting them, considering their value, need, usefulness, and frequency of use. From there I group things in common together and plan how they will fit back into the closet, allowing some space for new items. Despite the chaos, I'm reclassifying and evaluating.

Similarly, when we face changes in our lives, we start to examine what is valuable and true. What do we want to save—no matter how crowded the quarters? This is when we begin to live the words of Philippians 4:8. We concentrate our efforts on what is true and cast aside mistruths we have been storing inside. Focusing on what is noble, right, and pure, we discard what is petty, misguided, and impure.

This evaluation does not necessarily mean we throw away everything we previously based our behavior and decisions on. But we reach beyond what we knew before. We stretch our vision as we turn to God for direction.

And as we sort and discard, we may see how these decisions will bring added change to our lives. Friendships based on common ideas—ideas we are now setting aside—might be threatened. Our reputation might be called into question if we consider new viewpoints.

Have you ever walked into the home of someone who apparently never throws anything away? Contrarily, have you ever been to a junkyard and seen it as full of potential? Someone needs to say, "This could be of use—if it were repaired." A valuable painting hidden in the attic cannot be appreciated until it is dusted off and brought downstairs to be hung in a prominent place.

As you sort through your life, you may see some rubble—like that left in the wake of Hurricane Andrew. Use Philippians 4:8 as your guide. Be assured that "the peace of God will be with you."

———

Make a list of the dislocated emotions scattered about during your time of transition.

What items and issues need to be discarded or abandoned?

What needs repair?
> _____ emotions
> _____ relationships
> _____ attitudes
> _____ finances
> _____ beliefs
> _____ self-worth
> _____ other:

What needs to be preserved?

What help do you need? Where can you get it?

Chapter
· 5 ·

Soaring
Like Eagles

He gives strength to the weary
and increases the power of the weak.
Even youths grow tired and weary,
and young men stumble and fall;
but those who hope in the LORD
will renew their strength.
They will soar on wings like eagles;
they will run and not grow weary,
they will walk and not be faint.

Isaiah 40:29–31

WERE WE FACING change! After working at the same place for twenty-five years, my husband resigned. We were moving across the country—west to California.

I felt challenged, ready, eager, and prepared, and then I received a final promise from God. On our last Sunday morning, our beloved Pastor Ed opened his Bible and read the scripture on which he based his sermon.

Deuteronomy 33:25, "As your days, so shall your strength be" (NKJV). I can still hear his resonant voice. The sermon was energized with a special power that connected my heart with God's.

I was sure this move was God's will. We had prayed, waited, and worked through every detail with care and more prayer. Yet I was glad for the promise of added strength— should I need it.

How was I to know that the next few years were to be full of crisis, death, and defeat as well as added responsibility and pressure?

For years it seemed that every step I took in obedience to what I understood as God's will was challenged.

One tearful morning, wanting to run away, I turned to the Lord instead. I heard Him speak to my spirit: "As your days, so shall your strength be."

God is faithful to His Word. I knew that. Yes, He is faithful to His children, and I knew that, too. But that day I experienced the wonder of His faithfulness in a new way—to *me*.

The very moment I turned to wait on Him—to acknowledge my need of Him, He began to pour strength into me. He met me in crisis; He met me in pain; He met me in failure and in distress; He met me with strength, mercy, and love. Strength for each day, sleep for each night. As I faced public speaking engagements, I was aware that I was able to stand up in front of a group only because of His supernatural strength.

If we, you and me, will take a moment consciously to wait on the Lord—sit quietly before Him, especially during a time of awkward and difficult transition, we can experience refreshing renewal. We can be revitalized with the energy of a soaring eagle.

I still face challenges of change. There are still pressures, pain, and distress. I still find adjustments difficult and uncertainties unsettling. But, thankfully and with praise in my heart, I can also report there is still strength.

The promise I heard more than twelve years ago, I can still hear just as clearly today. My strength—His strength given to me—has equaled my days.

Even though I don't know what changes are challenging you, I do know that God has strength to offer you. Even if you are totally defeated—have given up—you can take the hope of His strength. Strength for this day, for this hour, right now—this very minute. Wait on the Lord. Take a deep breath, and imagine with that breath God pouring strength into you. Take it. Treasure it. Then use it.

Make a conscious effort to quiet yourself in the presence of the Lord for five uninterrupted minutes.

Now, fully aware of His presence, look at your life. What do you need God's strength to face?

If your challenge of change collided with God's strength and was infused with His power and wisdom, what decision would you make?

How would that change make today different and tomorrow different from yesterday?

Section II

Confronting Change

When you pass through the waters, I will be with you; and when you pass through the rivers, they will not sweep over you. When you walk through the fire, you will not be burned; the flames will not set you ablaze.

ISAIAH 43:2

CHANGE IS NEVER EASY. Getting from trauma or trepidation to victory may take a while—because it is a process.

"It's funny, the worst things I thought would happen if I moved across the country didn't. Even though I miss my old friends, I am not lonely and without friends."

"It's hard to believe, but this new job is not as intimidating as I thought it would be."

"Once I got through the enrollment process, I felt right at home on the campus and in the classes. I'm not the oldest one here after all and I really do remember how to study."

"Though many Christians warned me and disapproved of my decision, God hasn't cursed me for taking a stand against being abused. He hasn't abandoned me or deserted me because I chose not to submit or live any longer with a man who would tie me up and spit on me. In fact, my relationship with God is stronger than ever, and His love and care for me is evident every day as I walk through the daily difficulties of making it on my own."

Each of these women had a change of view—as she walked through change. In this section we will look at the process—how you can confront change one step at a time.

Chapter · 6 ·

Face Reality

By this time it was late in the day, so his disciples came to him. "This is a remote place," they said, "and it's already very late. Send the people away so they can go to the surrounding countryside and villages and buy themselves something to eat."

But he answered, "You give them something to eat."

They said to him, "That would take eight months of a man's wages! Are we to go and spend that much on bread and give it to them to eat?"

"How many loaves do you have?" he asked. "Go and see."

When they found out, they said, "Five—and two fish."

Mark 6:35–38

"HI, MOM. It's me, Sandy." I always welcome a phone call from my daughter—especially since we live more than three hundred miles apart.

"We have a little situation here," she said.

My spirits dampened a little. *Oh, boy,* I thought. *What now?*

"I'm pregnant again." I could hear an excitement in her

voice even though I was sure this baby was not planned and would change or delay certain goals she and her husband had set.

Actually, I could hear both joy and disappointment in my daughter's voice that day. She continued, acknowledging the inconvenience of the unexpected. "It will probably delay our move." But then she saw some very tangible positives—aside from the joy of new life. "But, then, maybe it'll be better to move a little later anyway. We have good insurance here, and we do have the cradle we can use again for a while."

Surprises come. We have our plans all set and something unexpected happens. We suddenly find ourselves shifting our focus, rearranging our priorities, and taking inventory of our resources.

That's what happened two thousand years ago, when a hungry crowd lingered after a long afternoon listening to Jesus speak. Feeling a responsibility toward the crowd, the disciples formed a committee and assessed the situation. It was late, and they were out in a deserted place. There was no way they could accommodate the need and feed the crowd. Their best bet was to dismiss the group and send them to fend for themselves. A very logical plan—or so they thought. They weren't really avoiding the situation; they were facing it as best they could.

When faced with our own challenges of change, it does no good to ignore the facts or deny the problems. You see, when the disciples brought the facts to Jesus, even Jesus didn't deny the problem, He simply had an unexpected solution.

"What resources do you have?" Jesus asked. Five loaves of bread and two little fish. I can almost imagine the disciples looking at the lunch-for-one and then scanning the great crowd of five thousand hungry people.

What can He do with five French rolls, a couple of carp, and a hungry mob? Maybe you have asked a similar question when you have looked at your resources and assessed your challenge.

You'll never know until you face the facts: the problem you have, the limit of your resources, the lack you face, and the solution only He can offer.

We often choose another way of dealing with our challenges. We don't face the facts; we ignore them. We disregard warnings or refuse to admit our problems. We expect miracles of deliverance but are afraid to articulate the need. We pray for God's intervention but never verbalize the problem.

The disciples didn't say, "Jesus, don't You see we have a problem here?" then wait for Him to guess what it was. They clearly stated the problem and proposed their solution. They even questioned His response. "Are You kidding? Do You know how much that would cost?"

Sometimes God says simply: Face reality. Only if you let Him bless what you have, will you see what He can do. And when it's all over, you may have more left over than when you started. To do that, you don't start with the blessing. You bring Him the burden. You can't realize the promise unless you are willing to face the problem. Only by giving Him the problem, along with the limited resources, can you realize the blessing of the leftovers.

———————

What realities do you need to face?

What resources do you have?

How do those resources compare to the reality of your need?

Write your realities on slips of paper and put them in an envelope. Write "my basket" on the outside. Then write your resources, your own solutions and suggestions, on other slips of paper and add them to the envelope. Now offer the "basket" (envelope) to Jesus. Ask Him to perform for you the same miracle He did for those five thousand people.

Write your prayer on another piece of paper, date it, and sign it. Now add it to the envelope. Put it in a safe place, where you put the other written exercises from this book. From time to time go back and review the items in the drawer. You will probably see changes taking place, not only in your situation, but also in *you*.

Chapter
· 7 ·

Confront Your
Anxieties

Then Esther sent this reply to Mordecai: "Go, gather together all the Jews who are in Susa, and fast for me. Do not eat or drink for three days, night or day. I and my maids will fast as you do. When this is done, I will go to the king, even though it is against the law. And if I perish, I perish."

Esther 4:15–16

THE YOUNG QUEEN ESTHER was the king's favorite. She had access to his palace. Servants were available to her night and day. She had the finest clothes and cosmetics. She had people assigned to entertain her, bathe, and feed her. She had free access to the palace and the king's resources, yet not to the king himself. She had limits and boundaries she was expected to live within.

To see the king, she was to wait until she was called for. Anyone, man or woman, who approached the king and came into the inner court without an invitation was doomed to death.

But Esther knew of a greater threat. The Jews—her own people—were scheduled for mass slaughter, extermination. As a Jew, Esther faced death if her national identity were made public. As the queen, she alone held the key to escape for her whole nation living with her in exile from their homeland. She had no time to wait for a kingly summons. She had to risk death to escape death. What a challenge!

Esther asked her people to fast. On the third day of the fast, she put on her royal robes and stood in the inner court of the palace, in a strategic place where the king could see her.

We know the end of the story, recorded in Scripture. But Esther had no way of knowing the consequences of her actions. Would stepping across the boundaries of protocol mean death or deliverance? She relied on her faith and spunk, using all the grit she could muster to do this gutsy thing. Quietly courageous, Esther became a magnificent heroine.

In a few simple words she announced her decision to face the challenge: "I will go to the king."

These words are acknowledged by scholars to be some of the bravest in the entire Bible.

Esther was faced with a challenge. She had a decision to make. Could she hide—go underground in the king's harem and hope she wouldn't be discovered—while her own people were slaughtered within hearing range of her bedroom? No. She felt she couldn't hide and turn away from the challenge set before her. Some things have to be faced and faced squarely —head on.

If you are to meet the challenge of your change, you will have to find the courage of Esther. Courage to face the anxiety of the unknown future.

It is of no use to hide our heads in the sand. We cannot hide from the changes ahead, nor can we escape their challenges. It's time to face the change. Avoidance will not help us make the difficult decisions or give us the courage we need. It's time we faced our future bravely and without wavering, knowing God will get us through.

———

When are you tempted to try to avoid the change ahead instead of face it?

Esther used a few well-chosen words to announce her decision to face the challenge: "I will go to the king." If you were to follow her example and make an announcement of your decision to face your challenge, how would you finish this sentence: "I will . . ."

What will you need?

_____ boldness
_____ bravery
_____ courage
_____ daring
_____ strength
_____ nerve
_____ grit
_____ willpower
_____ spunk
_____ other:

Esther did not have free access to her king; she took a great personal risk to enter his presence. However, we *have* free access to our King. We have an open invitation to enter His presence at any time. If you were to enter boldly into His presence and state your cause and make your requests, what would you say?

Chapter · 8 ·

Know That Some Things Never Change

"I the LORD do not change."

Malachi 3:6a

FOR ALL THE CHANGES I have chosen or been forced to make, there are certain things I can count on to stay the same.

Like what? Like the feeling I get each year when the winter winds change into warm spring breezes. Like the similar but different feeling I get each fall when the warm summer nights turn nippy and crisp with frost.

The same sense of hope returns year after year when daffodils and tulips fight their way up toward the sun, announcing that the earth is warming. Spring has sprung.

I always gasp with awe as I cross over the summit of Deadwood Ridge and let my eyes sweep across the lush valley floor and the majestic Sierras in the distance. I always smile with delight when I drive out to the apple farms when their trees are heavy with the early white blossoms promising an abundant fall harvest, or when I visit Pennsylvania while the maples burn with the bright colors of fall.

There's also a changeless quality of memory—especially when connected to the sense of smell. Can anyone in my generation forget the smell of Kresge's Five and Dime or of

49

the neighborhood meat market? I remember the familiar childhood smell of my grandma's purse and the tempting aroma of coffee brewing and bacon frying early in the morning. I remember the smell of apple cobbler, baked every Saturday, and pot roast, set on the table most every Sunday. I remember the smell of Grandpa's aftershave, and how the desert always smelled of sage and juniper after a rain. The ocean? Salt-water spray and tanning lotion. The movie theater? Popcorn.

Nothing has ever changed about the softness of a sleeping baby's cheek. Moms' shoulders still serve as pillows for pain, and Grandmas' laps are still shelters for little kids. Kittens are still soft and furry, and baby chickens warm and fuzzy.

The crunch of the first snow underfoot still makes many adults revert to childhood, and "The Star-Spangled Banner" played while the American flag waves over the head of an Olympic gold medalist still sends chills up spines.

Yes, it's true. While everything around us may seem as if it is changing, some things never change.

Jesus never changes. His love endures forever. His mercies are new every morning. His compassions never fail. His patience with me never wears thin. His forgiveness never runs out. His understanding is more than sufficient.

I guess of all the things that never change, I like Him the best. Don't you agree?

James 1:17: "Every good and perfect gift is from above, coming down from the Father of the heavenly lights, who does not change like shifting shadows."

Deuteronomy 33:27: "The eternal God is your refuge, and underneath are the everlasting arms."

Revelation 1:8: " 'I am the Alpha and the Omega,' says the Lord God, 'who is, and who was, and who is to come, the Almighty.' "

———————

What are some of your favorite "unchanging" things or memories?

How does hanging on to the "unchanging" help you to make the changes that must be made?

Chapter
· 9 ·

🌸 **Build New Security** 🌸

> *But now, this is what the LORD says—*
> *he who created you, O Jacob,*
> *he who formed you, O Israel:*
> *"Fear not, for I have redeemed you;*
> *I have summoned you by name; you are mine."*

Isaiah 43:1–2

YOU CAN DEPEND on God. It is so much easier to say it than to do it. And so much easier to do it when you don't have to. We have the assurance of His Word, the promise that He is there whenever we need Him. We know His love shelters and protects us, but . . .

Lillie's husband quit a secure job to open his own business. Rachel's husband left her. Margo, a single woman, recently changed jobs. Linda's house burned to the ground last month. Gloria decided to uproot and join her grown children in another state, leaving her friends and her church. Peggy's teenage son committed suicide, and Janine's son died of cancer in his senior year. Jackie, a woman with grown sons, has just borrowed enough money to go back to school and get her teaching certificate. Susan has decided to try to have another baby, even though her last one died suddenly in his crib. Kay's son was injured in a freak accident at a construction sight. Naomi's daughter was caught stealing, and Jerri is just realizing that her daughter is anorexic. Mary has discovered a lump in her breast.

People everywhere are making scary decisions and dealing with sudden changes. Christians hear from their friends, "Relax. Take it easy. You know God will see you through this." They tell stories of how God came through at the last minute, or they relay some miracle that occurred just in the nick of time. But for every story we hear of God's climactic rescue, there are countless others where the rescue didn't come and prayers seemingly were not answered. What happened to those people? Where was God then?

I have yet to hear anyone say that God let them down. Even when the worst possible thing happens, God's faithfulness is evident to those who are looking for it.

God is faithful to His people; God is faithful to you. You see, our ultimate security is not found in jobs, churches, or houses. It is not based on good health, a good marriage, or wonderful friends. Our security is not found in our children. It is found in the Lord and our belonging to Him.

"You are mine," He says in Isaiah 43. God takes care of what belongs to Him. No matter what.

If you are to base your security on Him, it will be because you choose to believe His Word, trust in what He says, and remain faithful to Him. We'll talk about this more later, but for now, start with the following statements based on God's Word. Read them and respond to them by writing your decision to believe that His faithfulness is stronger than your fear.

God is good to me.

Psalm 27:13: "I am still confident of this: I will see the goodness of the LORD in the land of the living."

I can trust God in this.

Jeremiah 17:7–8: "But blessed is the man who trusts in the LORD, whose confidence is in him. He will be like a tree planted by the water that sends out its roots by the stream. It does not fear when heat comes; its leaves are always green. It has no worries in a year of drought and never fails to bear fruit."

God is at work in my life.

Romans 8:28: "And we know that in all things God works for the good of those who love him, who have been called according to his purpose."

Proverbs 23:18: "There is surely a future hope for you, and your hope will not be cut off."

God has not forgotten me.

Jeremiah 29:11: " 'For I know the plans I have for you,' declares the LORD, 'plans to prosper you and not to harm you, plans to give you hope and a future.' "

I have a hopeful future.

Jeremiah 31:17: " 'So there is hope for your future,' declares the LORD. 'Your children will return to their own land.' "

I can trust God to work in me through this.

Job 23:10–12: "But he knows the way that I take; when he has tested me, I will come forth as gold. My feet have closely followed his steps; I have kept to his way without turning aside. I have not departed from the commands of his lips; I have treasured the words of his mouth more than my daily bread."

I have the assurance of His guidance.

Isaiah 30:21: "Whether you turn to the right or to the left, your ears will hear a voice behind you, saying, 'This is the way; walk in it.' "

My relationship with God is secure.

Romans 8:38–39: "For I am convinced that neither death nor life, neither angels nor demons, neither the present nor the future, nor any powers, neither height nor depth, nor anything else in all creation, will be able to separate us from the love of God that is in Christ Jesus our Lord."

———————

What are you facing today?

Write out what God is saying to you today about what new security you can find in His Word for your situation:

How can you be more faithful in your trust of God today?

Chapter · 10 ·

Celebrate the Possibilities

There is a time to weep and a time to laugh, a time to mourn and a time to dance.

Ecclesiastes 3:1, 4

"I'VE MADE UP my mind. I am going to file for divorce."

The agonizing decision was made alone in a hotel room. The young woman I was speaking to had called an end to her marriage after years of deception and abuse.

"How long has this been going on?" I asked.

"More than five years," she said. "I tried everything I knew to do. I tried not to push him. I tried to satisfy him. I 'submitted' and did things I felt in my heart were wrong because he wanted me to. But I can't anymore. I have asked him to go for counseling, and he says the problems are all mine. He doesn't want the pastor to know our problems, because then he will be so embarrassed he won't be able to go to church. He doesn't want me to talk to my friends about this, because then he won't be able to face them. I can't talk to his parents, because it isn't appropriate. He doesn't want me to go to mine, because it will cause permanent damage to his relationship with them. Yet he insists it's all my fault. But it's over. I've made my decision."

Sadly, the decision that will bring an end to the abuse has been laid on the victim. It was not an easy decision to make, and it will be even more difficult to live with.

She has chosen to alter, by taking drastic measures, the course of her life. With this decision, she is changing the course of her future and the future of her children. She will have to live with this decision and will somehow have to find the strength to meet the challenges this change will bring.

She will need to reorganize her priorities, make new friends, and shuffle her schedule until she finds stability again.

The challenges of her decision will require her attention, tax her strength, and test her faith. This is the most serious test she has faced so far in her young life. It will be difficult, to be sure, but she is already growing in and from the change. She is already meeting her challenge head on.

And as she sees small victories and major triumphs, she finds ways to celebrate. Yes, celebrate.

"One thing I am celebrating," she says, "is the return of my self-respect. Also, the freedom to make small decisions without the fear of criticism—what I wear, how long I stay in the shower, what color I paint my nails, how I style my hair. I can cook what I choose, vacuum after the kids are in bed, and strip the wallpaper I never liked from the bathroom.

"I am celebrating my ability to solve problems. I have dealt with unruly children. I have handled my car breaking down. I'm scheduling baby-sitters and am juggling work and home responsibilities.

"I have also made decisions to forgive and have decided to find the strength to overcome the temptation to become bitter. I have chosen to keep a regular quiet time and stay close in my relationship with God.

"I have supportive friends. I'm considering returning to school and have found many programs that help women in my situation. And, of course, I have my kids. They alone give me reason to celebrate."

Another woman told me, "I didn't ask for this change. I didn't want it, but it's what I got. When my whole life was shattered, I decided it was best to pick up what pieces I had left and go on to new things rather than sit amid the ruin. All in all, my life is pretty great now, just the way it is."

You might not be at that point yet. But you can look back over the last month, week, or day, and ask God to show you one reason to celebrate.

The situation you face today may present some problems, but it no doubt also presents some possibilities. Name three opportunities your problem presents to you:

How can you celebrate those possibilities?

Name three ways in which you are stronger because you have gone through a particular time of change:

How can you celebrate the ways in which you have grown?

Section III

Anchored
in the
God of Hope

May the God of hope fill you with all joy and peace as you trust in him, so that you may overflow with hope by the power of the Holy Spirit.

ROMANS 15:13

CHANGE IS BOUND to come. Change is bound to go. And more change is bound to follow. But one thing is sure: our Lord, whom Paul describes as "the God of hope." The traditional symbol for hope is an anchor. That biblical metaphor is used in Hebrews 6:19: "We have this hope as an anchor for the soul, firm and secure."

For an anchor to hold us secure in a storm, we must be firmly connected to that anchor. The next five chapters give principles for holding on to the anchor of hope. These five principles deal directly with our relationship to God.

Principle 1:
Read
God's Word
Daily

The LORD is a refuge for the oppressed, a stronghold in times of trouble. Those who know your name will trust in you, for you, LORD, have never forsaken those who seek you.

Psalm 9:9–10

NOTHING SQUEEZES the hope out of me faster than feeling oppressed by circumstances. Some situations seem overwhelming even though I have a glimpse of the long-term plan and benefits. I can be tempted to despair even when I am sure that in six months life will be right again. Why is that? Because it isn't the long-term change that threatens my hope as much as the short-term transition.

Let me use another analogy to describe the trauma of transition. It is like shooting the rapids in a rubber raft. You have a goal: to arrive downstream without being thrown from the boat. But getting there—what a ride! Each turn in the course requires constant paddling, maneuvering, shifting. And of course you're depending on the guide who has been down the river countless times before.

If you think of your transition as a raft ride down a rapid river, think of God as your guide. While He is there to get you safely to your destination, He puts a paddle in your hand and expects you to participate. His Word is that paddle—that which you hang on to and use to progress toward your goal.

God's timeless Word speaks to every generation—to every individual and to every situation.

The verses above teach us that God is a refuge, a stronghold in just such times as you are facing. His Word tells us that God can be trusted; He is someone we can depend on for stability and hope. It tells us that we can depend on Him never to forsake us. He is our refuge.

Strong's Exhaustive Concordance says that the *refuge* of Psalm 9 literally means "cliff, or other lofty or inaccessible high place."

This does not mean that God is lofty or inaccessible, but that when we run to Him for safety, He puts us in a place where nothing can hurt or harm us.

Does that mean that all your troubles will just go away? No, of course not. It means that you can be in such a place that the trouble you are facing, the transitions you are being required to make, will not devastate you or deter you from your goal of spiritual and personal growth.

You might feel the discomfort or even pain, but when God is your refuge, this transition does not have to leave any destructive residue or bitterness in your heart and life. You can be safe from damage. You may be exposed to the suffering, but saved from destruction. Don't expect God to take you out of the situation, but hope in Him to take you through it.

When you read the Word of God every day, holding on to such verses, you have hope—hope based on God's unchangeable Word. That wooden paddle isn't going to do you any good if it's left on the bank of the river or if it lies in the bottom of the raft. Pick up your paddle. Take your responsibility for hanging on to the one sure thing He offers you—himself, revealed through the pages of His Word.

Maintaining your hope requires the discipline of being a daily Bible reader. Read a verse, a chapter, or an entire book—the length of the passage doesn't really matter—until your hope is rekindled and your goals are clearly within sight once again.

God waits to be your strong tower, your refuge. Hope in Him. He will never disappoint you. The Bible tells us so.

What deters you from reading the Bible every day?

What motivates you to embrace the discipline of daily Bible reading?

What changes can you make to your schedule to provide the time you need for daily Bible reading?

_____ setting the alarm thirty minutes earlier
_____ using your break time at work
_____ turning off the TV, or not turning it on in the morning
_____ other:

What preparations can you make to help you keep your new commitment to maintaining a daily quiet time?

_____ laying out your Bible the night before, open to the passage you want to read

_____ getting a daily Bible reading guide at the bookstore or at church

_____ joining a Bible study that requires a certain amount of daily homework

_____ other:

Choose one passage of hopeful scripture and meditate on it today.

Chapter
· 12 ·

Principle 2:
Keep Your
Focus

*"Thou wilt keep him in perfect peace, whose mind is
stayed on thee; because he trusteth in thee."*

Isaiah 26:3 (KJV)

"WHERE CAN I GO to find the hope that lasts?" Haven't
we all asked that question?

Those of us who have experienced financial reversals, re-
bellion in our teenaged children, or family health problems
have often sought the Lord for hope. Life's ups and downs can
be very threatening—even appear hopeless—especially when
they steal our attention and divert our focus away from God's
Word.

Once my eighteen-year-old daughter told me that she
never wanted to talk to me again. She made it clear that she
wanted me to forget I ever knew her. For months she grieved
me with her bitterness, stabbed me with her words—and her
silences—and shattered me with her coldness.

But now, six years later, our relationship has been restored.
We are closer than I ever dared to imagine or hope for. Certainly she lives with her own regrets, as do I. But we have
made a commitment to each other and have promised to speak
only words that build our relationship, not destroy it. We have

learned to confront our differences without battling each other.

Now I look back on those heartbreaking days. Faced with hopelessness, I was tempted to focus on the hurt or on reexamining my mothering methods, trying to figure out where I went wrong. But I learned to discipline my thoughts and turn them to hope. I learned what it means to keep my mind stayed on Christ.

The King James translation of Isaiah 26:3 is so familiar: "Thou wilt keep him in perfect peace, whose mind is stayed on thee; because he trusteth in thee." Other versions of the Bible give more insight into this principle for maintaining hope:

The Amplified Bible: "You will guard him and keep him in perfect and constant peace whose mind [both its inclination and its character] is stayed on You, because he commits himself to You, leans on You and hopes confidently in You."

The New American Standard Bible: "The steadfast of mind Thou wilt keep in perfect peace, because he trusts in Thee."

New International Version: "You will keep in perfect peace him whose mind is steadfast, because he trusts in you."

The mind stayed on God our Father, renewed in His Word, given revelation of Christ through that Word, and empowered by the Holy Spirit is the mind that is promised peace.

I learned not to focus my mind on the hurt, but neither did I "visualize" or "imagine" my daughter whole and restored. I learned to keep my mind focused on Christ and His love for me and my daughter.

This does not mean that we neglect our responsibilities and fill our minds with pictures of heaven, imagining the face of Jesus in the clouds. No, we do give attention to our situations, but we don't totally focus on the problem—on our own pain. As we fix our mind on Him, we find peace, and with the peace, strength.

Keeping a clear focus on Him is what helps us to keep on working, worshiping, serving, and, in the case of my relationship with my daughter, loving.

Do you need hope? This is the solution:

Choose to fix your mind on Christ—not the change, not

the transition, but on Him. Let your thoughts drift toward Him instead of being driven toward and riveted on your problems. Allow your spirit to rise to the Father in wonderful communion, opening communication with Him that is often too deep for words.

Fix your mind on Him,
    on His love,
        on His mercy,
            and His faithfulness.
Focus on Him
    and His provision,
        His abundance.
Experience His joy,
    His peace,
        and hope.

What problems have you been focusing on?

_____ financial
_____ a child or children
_____ family relationships
_____ your marriage
_____ your work
_____ your church
_____ strained friendship(s)
_____ guilt
_____ temptations
_____ failure
_____ past hurts
_____ physical problems
_____ depression
_____ the need for direction
_____ the need for love
_____ the need for friends
_____ confusion
_____ anger
_____ loneliness
_____ unforgiveness
_____ other:

Take the above checked-off list and hold it up before God. In a prayer of commitment, give these problems into His care. Pray this suggested prayer:

"Heavenly Father, I surrender. I give up. I cannot handle the pressures of these problems any longer. The answer must come from You. You alone are able to take care of all the situations that threaten me. I trust in You. I love You. I am Your child and I need Your help. Please give me the strength to focus my attention on You instead of my circumstances. Give me a new perspective. Give me a new revelation of You. My decision today is to "stay my mind" on You. I praise You for who You are. You have done for me what I have needed most; You have given me a relationship with You, through Jesus, in whose name I pray. Father, thank You for helping me focus my mind and maintain hope. Amen."

Chapter
· 13 ·

Principle 3:
Maintain a Vital Prayer Life

Then Jesus told his disciples a parable to show them that they should always pray and not give up.

Luke 18:1

THE PARABLE JESUS told is sometimes called "The Parable of the Persistent Widow." In this story a persevering woman gives an apathetic judge a chronic pain in the neck. This woman had a request and kept badgering him. She had a need that only the judge could meet, and she was not to be put off. She knew her rights and would not be deterred by the cold, stony-hearted judge.

Finally he gives in. "Though I don't fear God or care about men, yet because this widow keeps bothering me, I will see that she gets justice, so that she won't eventually wear me out with her coming!" (Luke 18:4–5).

Jesus makes a spiritual parallel with this parable. We can be like the widow. His lesson is about the importance of persistence in prayer. It's not a reflection of God's character as "the judge." In fact, He makes His point using an illustration based on opposites. The earthly judge is cold, unfeeling, and unmoved until the widow wears him down. He grants her request only because he is tired of her hounding.

But God, the righteous Judge, does not have to be worn down. He does not answer our prayers because He is weary of our petitions or tired of us coming to Him again and again. You see, our persistence in prayer does not change God, nor does it change His mind. Persistence changes us. It produces consistency.

Praying is hard work. It is easier to see our need for prayer than it is to pray for our needs. That's why we make our prayer requests to our pastors or friends, to our prayer groups, and even to Mom.

Yet prayer is as essential to the victorious Christian life as good dental hygiene is to the health of our teeth. To keep our teeth in good condition, we see the professionals on a regular basis. But the daily care—brushing, flossing, and eating a good diet—is our responsibility.

It is good for us to seek prayer support, but if we do so in place of regular, private prayer with our Lord, it's as if we are asking someone else to brush our teeth.

As you persist in your personal prayer life, remember these four important things God wants to say to you:

1. *I am here.* "Then you will call, and the LORD will answer; you will cry for help, and he will say: Here am I" (Isaiah 58:9).

2. *I will hear you.* "Before they call I will answer; while they are still speaking I will hear" (Isaiah 65:24).

3. *I will answer.* "I will refine them like silver and test them like gold. They will call on my name and I will answer them; I will say, 'They are my people,' and they will say, 'The LORD is our God' " (Zechariah 13:9).

4. *I will act.* "If you remain in me and my words remain in you, ask whatever you wish, and it will be given you" (John 15:7).

If you will maintain your hope during this challenge of change, it will not be because you concentrate on maintaining hope, but because you determine to maintain a consistent and vital prayer life—communing with God, not just nagging him.

Why is your prayer life so important? Because hope placed in that which we hope for is not substantial; it has no substance. But hope placed in God, through daily communication, through prayer, is substantial—because God is.

76

Are you more likely to take your needs to God or to someone else as prayer requests? Why?

When is it good to seek prayer and ministry from others?

Give a personal example of persistence in action. Then apply that picture of persistence to your own prayer life.

But as for me, I will always have hope; I will praise you more and more.

Psalm 71:14

IF I BECOME a "praiser" am I gonna get weird? You might know people who bowl others over with their constant praises to God. Their spiritual sounds and words lose their meaning because of overuse.

But such extreme examples are no excuse for holding ourselves back from living a life of praise.

Yes, we can live as well as speak our praises. How? With attitudes of respect and regard for sacred things. When we esteem one another, we praise God. When we appreciate those in authority and submit one to another out of respect, our lives are a testimony of praise.

When we speak with reverence about God, we praise Him. When we acknowledge His care and love, talk about His wonders and works, we praise Him.

There are also times when it is appropriate to lift our voices in direct praise to God our Father and Jesus our King. When we express our love to Him, we are praising Him. When our adoration for Him cries out to find verbal expression and our heart discovers a need to applaud Him, we can't help but praise Him.

Sometimes, when my heart is overflowing, I sing repetitious praise choruses I learned at church, like: "I Stand in Awe of You" or "Majesty, Worship His Majesty." They help me to capture just a glimpse of the King of Kings and Lord of Lords deep within me. "In the Presence of a Holy God" invokes an awareness of the Ruler of the universe standing here in my house, in this very room, with me—of all people, me!

David—a man who knew all about the trauma of transition and change—knew what it was to lift up his praises to God. The Book of Psalms is filled with praises that we can read and make our own, when we can't find the words we long to speak.

He wrote: "I will exalt you, my God the King; I will praise your name for ever and ever. Every day I will praise you and extol your name for ever and ever. Great is the LORD and most worthy of praise; his greatness no one can fathom" (Psalm 145:1–3).

Praising God helps connect us to that anchor of hope. In times of turmoil praise gives a solid footing and helps us keep our balance. When change threatens to overwhelm, praise gives birth to an awareness of Someone bigger, who chooses to be involved with me and my challenges and assures me and gives me hope.

But the best reason of all to praise God is this: He is worthy of our praise, more worthy of our praise than our challenge of change is worthy of our worry.

No, you don't have to get weird. But wouldn't it be nice to be different?

When is it the easiest to praise God? Take one of your worries and turn it into praise.

Read Psalm 145:1–146:2. Highlight or copy down every word, phrase, or sentence that applies to your life as well as to David's.

If you were to write a prayer or song of praise using words you rarely use, what would you say? Write that prayer here:

Principle 5:
Trust the Lord

But I trust in you, O LORD;
I say, "You are my God."
My times are in your hands.

Psalm 31:14–15a

DADDY LIFTS his little girl so she is standing on the kitchen countertop. Stepping back a bit, he holds out his hands. "Jump," he says.

She hesitates. Daddy seems so far away. She waits, wanting him to move closer. Daddy moves just slightly toward her and repeats the command. "Jump."

She searches his face, looks into his eyes. Could Daddy be serious? He's smiling. It's a crazy thing for him to ask, but the memory of other times—being held safely in those out-stretched arms—gives her confidence. And his kisses that have healed her "owies." She knows his love.

But the gap is so wide! Daddy is a full six inches away. Maybe if he were just a little closer. She crouches and reaches as far as her little arms will allow, hoping he will reach toward her even more.

Daddy, coaxing her to jump, understands her anxiety. "Come on," he urges. "I'll catch you."

Crouching even more, she leans forward and stretches out her hand. Her wide eyes and tense body beg Daddy to touch her.

She drops her eyes toward the floor. "Fall." Her concern is expressed in that one word.

"No you won't," Daddy reassures. "I won't let you fall. Come on, jump."

She withdraws her hands and clutches her stomach. Once again she leans forward, stretches out her arms, and this time she slowly allows herself to fall into Daddy's waiting arms. Before her little feet can leave the counter, her father scoops her up and swings her around with laughter and congratulations. They both let out whoops of delight.

Holding her close, he covers her cheeks with kisses, sets her on the counter again, and the game goes on.

This time the child hesitates only slightly and soon is leaping into her father's outstretched arms.

I remember this little ritual between my husband and daughter, and I imagine it repeated in every generation. It illustrates the psalmist's words, "I trust in you, O LORD; I say 'You are my God.' My times are in your hands."

I see the scenario repeated in my own adult life. I have been like my little daughter, Sandy, although rather than on the countertop, I have been on the edge of a circumstance or new experience. Aware of my own inadequacy and helplessness, I have cried to God, "Help me. Get me out of this!"

And I've heard Him answer, "Stretch and jump."

I have hesitated, afraid, yet wanting to trust. I've always known I could trust God, but I've wanted to learn to trust Him in new ways. I would take those little six-inch jumps into the steady, outstretched arms. After a while I became more comfortable with faith until it almost became a game.

But let me return to my daughter's story. One day there was a new twist added to the game in the kitchen.

"Jump," Daddy commanded.

"No," was the response.

"Jump," he repeated.

"No."

Daddy put his hands on his hips while Sandy stifled a giggle. "Sandy," he said firmly, "I said jump."

84

Still giggling, she turned her back to her father.

"Okay," he warned, "you'll just have to stay there."

She peeked over her shoulder.

Daddy stepped back and turned to walk out of the kitchen.

"Daddy?" She waited. "Daddy!" she cried. "Jump, Daddy, jump!" She stretched out her little arms as far as she could toward him.

Daddy looked over his shoulder, waited for a moment, testing her seriousness, then he moved toward her.

She crouched.

He moved closer.

Her whole body strained to reach him. She was nearly in tears.

As he approached she threw herself into his arms.

There was not the same joy in this jump. She fastened her arms tightly around her daddy's neck, and he carried her into the living room. Each time he tried to put her down, she clung to him. She needed to know his closeness, be reassured by his love. He held her, smoothed her hair, and eventually she slept in his lap.

———

One day, the issue of trust wasn't a game with me anymore. About the time I felt strong and in control and flaunted my self-sufficiency—I "knew" God would be there for me—I experienced a brush with death.

The terror that was in Sandy's eyes was suddenly in mine. Was God going to catch me or leave me stranded? "God, I won't play games with You. Are You there? Have You abandoned me?"

Are you afraid that God might abandon you at a stage of change in your life? Are you needing His reassurance, even though you've taken His care for granted? If so, all you need to do is stretch out your faith and trust toward Him. Jump! He will catch you. He is a faithful Father. You will be held within the warm circle of His love where you can rest and feel secure.

Know for yourself what it means to say, "I trust in you, O LORD; I say 'You are my God.' My times are in your hands."

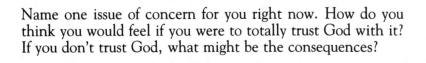

Name one issue of concern for you right now. How do you think you would feel if you were to totally trust God with it? If you don't trust God, what might be the consequences?

If you have decided to completely trust Him, write out what you will say to Him, affirming that trust.

Read Psalm 121:2–8. Pick out one or two phrases and meditate on them throughout the day.

Section IV

Anchored
in a
Community of Hope

Two are better than one, because they have a good return for their work: If one falls down, his friend can help him up. But pity the man who falls and has no one to help him up!

ECCLESIASTES 4:9–10

SECTION III was focused on maintaining hope by maintaining a solid relationship with God. That relationship is of primary importance to us as believers. But the Bible is full of admonition to the church of Christ. We are a *body* of believers—each part connected to and in need of the others.

As we reach out to other people, especially other Christians, we receive encouragement, stability; new insights that give us a clearer perspective on our strengths and weaknesses, failures and successes, problems and promises.

This section, "Anchored in a Community of Hope," focuses on our need for human relationships. They help us maintain hope and teach us how to persevere in times of change and challenge.

Chapter · 16 ·

Principle 6: Worship With Other Believers

Speak to one another with psalms, hymns and spiritual songs.

Ephesians 5:19

Let us not give up meeting together, as some are in the habit of doing, but let us encourage one another—and all the more as you see the Day approaching.

Hebrews 10:25

ONE HAS ONLY TO TRAVEL a short distance on our elaborate network of freeways to see signs of togetherness. Signs announcing "Park and Ride," "Ridesharing," and "Vanpools" encourage people to leave their personal car behind and ride with another whenever possible.

There are benefits to being together besides the obvious ones—less confusion on the already overcrowded highway system, less air pollution, carpool lane privileges, etc. There are also the emotional benefits—just being together with other people.

However, for all its benefits, the American way is the way of independence. Even when it has been proven to be beneficial, if being part of the group means even a slight sacrifice of personal wishes, an adjustment to schedules or the slightest inconvenience, many Americans still choose to go it alone.

Unfortunately, there are Christians who carry the American way of individuality and independence into their worship experience as well.

Not fully understanding that the worship expression is to be a corporate expression, at least a good part of the time, many deceive themselves into believing that a lonely, individual, independent worship experience is just as, if not more valid. Don't misunderstand me, there are times when it is appropriate, even necessary to worship alone. But that is not to be the whole worship experience.

God designed humans to live in the context of relationships—with Him and with each other. We are also designed to worship in the context of relationship.

When the stresses of a sick baby, troubled teenager, and personal health have discouraged me the most, I found strength and hope while attending corporate worship services. When life took an unexpected turn and personal failure seemed to threaten my life with uncertainty, the corporate worship of my church gave me a place to experience the security, the dependability of God's presence.

It's so good to meet with other believers when I am weak. I blend my weak voice with theirs, and together we find strength. When I lay my own agenda aside, submit to the leadership of my church, absorb the energy generated from Christians sitting close to me, and let my spirit soar in worship there is peace—wonderful peace. Peace coming from our Father-God visiting His worshiping children with His presence.

What personal sacrifices do you have to make to meet in corporate worship?

_____ music style preference
_____ schedule
_____ sermon length
_____ temperature in church building
_____ someone sitting in your seat

_____ sitting alongside hypocrites

_____ possibility of facing someone who has hurt your feelings

_____ uncomfortable chairs or pews

_____ other:

Think back to your past—more than a year ago. How has the church community in a worship or study setting helped you maintain your hope?

Think of your current worship environment. As you face new challenges of change, what can you do to make yourself more open to God's healing and steadying hand?

Chapter
· 17 ·

Principle 7:
Work Humbly
Alongside
Other Believers

*Clothe yourselves with humility toward one
another. . . . Humble yourselves, therefore, under God's
mighty hand, that he may lift you up in due time. . . .
Be self-controlled and alert. Your enemy the devil
prowls around like a roaring lion looking for someone to
devour.*

1 Peter 5:5b, 6, 8

WE DID IT! Standing together, working side by side, we built a new church. We learned to hang Sheetrock and handle screw guns. We learned to wrap heating and air conditioning ducts. We wore protective masks and sanded cement floors until they were as smooth as glass. Then we learned to lay flooring. We painted, papered, and put in ceiling tiles. Our hands got rough and calloused as we raked, swept, sanded, and nailed.

We gave of our time—sacrificed Saturdays and vacations—and we gave of our financial resources. But, best of all, we gave of ourselves.

We let major home projects wait until the church building was finished. We put our own interests aside while we focused on our communal project.

And the most amazing thing happened. While we were building a building, God was building His Church. Not the building—us. What do I mean, exactly? We became friends. We learned about one another's families; we learned who works well together; we began to care about one another in the most wonderful ways.

Well, most of us did, anyway. There were a few stragglers who felt that giving up a Saturday now and then was an imposition. They stood at a distance and criticized the workmanship of the volunteers, the color of the roof, or the size of the fellowship hall. They pouted when they thought the volunteer workers got too much of the pastor's time and attention. How sad—and how dangerous.

Dangerous? Yes, it can be dangerous. Let me explain. First Peter 5 was written to a church—a church much like mine, even like yours. Here young men were instructed to be submissive to the older, and the entire church—called "God's flock"—was admonished to be humble, self-controlled, and alert. "Clothe yourselves with humility toward one another" (v. 5). "Be self-controlled and alert" (v. 8).

You see, there was an enemy of the flock—the Devil. Like a roaring lion, he was roaming around seeking someone to devour (v. 8). Not a group, not a church, not even the whole flock—but someone. Can you see the picture? There are certain ones of the flock who were most vulnerable.

The stragglers. The enemy doesn't usually attack the group as a whole, but one at a time. And one straggling behind is an easy target.

But we don't have to be isolated loners. We don't have to be cut off. We can make an effort to belong. In finding our place in the flock, we can find a wonderful dimension of Christian living that makes us "strong, firm and steadfast" (v. 10).

"For where two or three come together in my name, there am I with them," says Jesus in Matthew 18:20. I think He not only refers to worship and study groups, but also to groups of Christians who are working and playing together.

I remember seeing a line of kindergarten children on a field trip to the library. From a distance I saw that they walked in perfect order, evenly spaced with a teacher in front and a teacher behind. Amazing! Not until I got much closer did I discover that they were holding a small rope tied with knots at eighteen-inch intervals. That's what it's like to belong: each of us in humility and self-control willing to hold the rope at our designated knot.

Consider maintaining your hope by holding on to your knot, staying with the group for safety and security. Don't struggle for someone else's place. There is room for everyone. We are part of the body of Christ; we are in this together. Since we are part of each other, it seems a good idea to stay together.

When have you been a straggler?

What can you do to make sure you are safe in the middle of the flock?

How can that position help you to have and maintain your hope?

Chapter
· 18 ·

Principle 8:
**Be Careful
With Whom
You Share**

*After six days Jesus took with him Peter, James and
John the brother of James, and led them up a high
mountain by themselves.*

Matthew 17:1

*He did not say anything to them without using a
parable. But when he was alone with his own disciples,
he explained everything.*
*That day when evening came, he said to his disciples,
'Let us go over to the other side.' Leaving the crowd
behind, they took him along, just as he was, in the boat.*

Mark 4:34–36

TOGETHERNESS AND CORPORATE cohesiveness is
great. It strengthens us, and it makes for healthy churches and
Bible study groups. But as wonderful as togetherness is, it
should not be confused with intimacy.

How many times have you been in a small-group discussion
and cringed as someone shared a painful incident in their life
that was so intimate it made you uncomfortable? It is easy to
see that in another setting, perhaps alone with the hurting
person, you wouldn't have felt so ill-at-ease.

Intimacy shared in an open group setting can undermine the purpose of the group as well as the effort on the part of the wounded to share. It can even fracture the group and consequently destroy the fellowship. When that happens, hope of healing and working through a threatening change can be delayed, and disappointment can set in.

As Christians, it is important that we learn how to have fellowship with many, but be intimate with only a few.

Jesus knew that principle. He spoke to the crowds in parables. As He told stories, He knew that some would be able to draw the spiritual parallels and make the applications. But then He drew aside a few disciples and shared with them in greater depth. Through His explanations on a more intimate level, He drew them closer to himself and closer to one another.

There are many reasons for not sharing intimacies with a large group. Here are a few of the more obvious reasons:

1. *Some within a group cannot handle hearing the deep struggles of others.* Perhaps they are new Christians; hearing about the doubts of others will feed their own. They simply are not ready.

2. *Some hearers will be untrustworthy.* A few may not have learned the importance of trust, of keeping in confidence things shared in a group. This is often how destructive rumors begin.

3. *A group setting doesn't give the personal help that is needed for a private problem.* Those closest to us will give us the insight we need and hold us accountable. If we share openly with a large group, a variety of solutions are open to discussion and it is easy to become confused.

4. *A secret told is no longer a secret.* Revealing too much of our private lives to a general group of people is inappropriate. It almost guarantees that our secret will be misunderstood by someone and we will get hurt in the long run.

Of course there are times when open, honest, forthright sharing *is* appropriate, when the information shared is not of a private or intimate nature. In fact, it is essential to learn to share if we are to become healthy, hopeful individuals. In the next chapter we will discuss this further.

Can you recall a time when something was shared inappropriately in a group?

Can you recall when a prayer request was given that was of an intimate nature? How could that request have been handled differently?

Have you ever sacrificed the joy of togetherness because you were afraid you would be "forced" to share something you were not ready to share? Was your fear reasonable or do you think you were overly cautious?

Chapter
· 19 ·

Principle 9:
Get a Partner

Two are better than one,
because they have a good return for their work:
If one falls down,
his friend can help him up.
But pity the man who falls
and has no one to help him up!
Also, if two lie down together, they will keep warm.
But how can one keep warm alone?
Though one may be overpowered,
two can defend themselves.
A cord of three strands is not quickly broken.

Ecclesiastes 4:9–12

WE LIVE IN an increasingly complex society. Most of us operate in a constant state of hurry, and despite a houseful of work-saving appliances, find our schedules more crowded than ever. We can meet more people and travel more miles in a day than our great-grandparents did in a lifetime.

Yet despite the active social whirl and intense busyness, loneliness is on the upsurge. Why? Because while we may know more people, we most likely have fewer friends—those who are honest with us and love us without condition; people who demand nothing from us, but expect and hope for our best; those who listen to us and try to empathize with our pain.

But hopefully one or two people, maybe even three exceptional people find a special place in our hearts and lives. They become rare treasures of hope and support. They are our true friends.

Close friends help us to overcome our obstacles through encouragement and caring confrontation. Friends walk alongside us and whisper words of reassurance, cheer us on to our goals. Friends remain strong in faith when ours is weak. Friends let us rest, without criticizing us for not doing more. Friends stand beside us when we are tempted. Friends pray for us when we forget to pray for ourselves; give us advice when we ask for it and wisely refrain when we don't.

Yes, such friendships are rare—but essential for sustaining life and hope.

I have a few close friends—only a few. They are my life-hope support system. They are my partners.

These intimate friends actually personify Philippians 2:4: "Each of you should look not only to your own interests, but also to the interests of others." And also 2 John 1:5–6: "And now, dear lady, I am not writing you a new command but one we have had from the beginning. I ask that we love one another. And this is love: that we walk in obedience to his commands. As you have heard from the beginning, his command is that you walk in love."

What about you? Can you say the same? Do you have such a friend? Are you such a friend?

———

Name your three closest friends:

1.

2.

3.

Remembering particular incidents, tell how each of the friends you've listed fits the description of Ecclesiastes 4:9–12.

How have you fit that same description for someone else?

If you aren't able to identify a close friend or partner, perhaps some pain that you hold too closely keeps you from having close friends.

Is there such pain in your life?

If friendship is something you desire and value, what can you do to make or keep a few good friends?

Chapter
• 20 •

Principle 10:
**Find Where
You Fit**

> *Now the body is not made up of one part but of
> many. If the foot should say, "Because I am not a hand,
> I do not belong to the body," it would not for that reason
> cease to be part of the body. And if the ear should say,
> "Because I am not an eye, I do not belong to the body,"
> it would not for that reason cease to be part of the body.
> If the whole body were an eye, where would the sense of
> hearing be? If the whole body were an ear, where would
> the sense of smell be? But in fact God has arranged the
> parts in the body, every one of them, just as he wanted
> them to be. If they were all one part, where would the
> body be? As it is, there are many parts, but one body.
> The eye cannot say to the hand, "I don't need you!"
> And the head cannot say to the feet, "I don't need you!"
> Now you are the body of Christ, and each one of you
> is a part of it.*

1 Corinthians 12:14–21, 27

AS WE FACE change, our faith—and hope—is fortified as
we see our place in the body of Christ. Do you worship each
Sunday, even occasionally work or play with church people,
and yet still not feel as if you really fit in?

You can make the difference between feeling that you fit or feeling like a misfit. Yes, that's right, *you*. You can help yourself to have the security of belonging somewhere. And security gives hope; it eases the insecurity of change.

You can feel like an outsider at work, a bother to the family, and an outcast at church. Or you can be a part of the "inner circle" where things are happening. And it mostly depends on you.

All of us send off certain signals—our attitudes, our behavior, and our willingness or unwillingness to be a part. Those attitudes and behaviors make themselves evident because we don't know our own gifts, or when we do, we're not willing to submit them for the good of the group.

I know an intelligent woman who consistently sends unfriendly signals. She rarely participates as a part of the team, preferring to stay in her own distant and independent world. She no doubt has many good qualities and talents, but, sad to say, we probably will never know what they are.

My efforts to draw her into the circle have been rebuffed time and again. Others have reported the same response. She never laughs and hardly ever speaks to anyone.

Pain, someone said, she must be carrying pain, and we must prove our love for her and be patient. Insecurity, offered another. She is insecure and we must prove ourselves as safe. Lack of trust, suggested a third. She is unable to trust us, and we must be able to prove ourselves trustworthy. Someone else thinks the woman doesn't think anyone cares about her and so keeps to herself. If we could just find a way to prove we care.

I think it is none of the above. My personal opinion is that she is either nursing a past pain and has become comfortable with it, or she has not taken recent inventory of her gifts and actively sought places where those gifts could be offered and used.

We could assure her of those gifts, but she probably wouldn't believe us. We could go out of our way to include her, and she would discount our efforts as empty and suspect. We could make our best promises and perform until we were exhausted. I expect her attitude wouldn't change. I believe she has decided not to be included; she has chosen to make no effort to find out where she fits or to make the effort to fill that place.

Where you fit may not be immediately obvious. For about five years every church job that suited my evident gifts was filled with someone more gifted and adequate. I didn't teach a class, sing in the choir, or even hand out bulletins on Sunday mornings.

Since I have usually been active in leadership or teaching, this was a rare time in my life. I could have chosen to be insecure, whine, or pout. I could have run to another church, but I chose to accept this as God's plan for me for the time being. And while my inactivity seemed awkward at first, this soon became a very special time.

Feeling God's direction simply to be supportive and steady, I looked for creative ways to do that. I sent cards and notes of encouragement to those who were active and visible. I made it a habit to offer appreciation to the church janitor. I made it a point to notice when the lawn was freshly mowed and manicured. I offered a compliment to the soloist. I wrote letters to the pastor, explaining how I applied the sermon to my life and how I appreciated his study and prayerful preparation. I caught the eyes of children and smiled at them or touched their shoulders briefly in passing. Happy and secure, I hugged anyone, smiled at everyone.

I don't know when I ever "did less" in the church. At the same time, I don't know if I've ever felt as if I fit in more. I was in God's place, doing what He called me to do.

Those days are past and I have resumed leadership responsibilities. But there is a change in me. I have a new appreciation for help, dedication, and teamwork. I appreciate effort and commitment. I like people better. I like myself better. I fit. And when I fit, I belong, and when I belong, I have hope.

How about you? Do you have a place where you fit?

––––––––––

Place your level of giftedness on a scale of one to ten:

_____ Nothing to give
_____ Average level of abilities
_____ Above average

If you say you have nothing to give I must warn you, I believe even a person who only knows how to smile has something to give. And how can you show more support for those who do have a lot to give? Isn't showing support a gift?

What gift have you been hiding and why?

How does offering that gift carry the possibility of belonging?

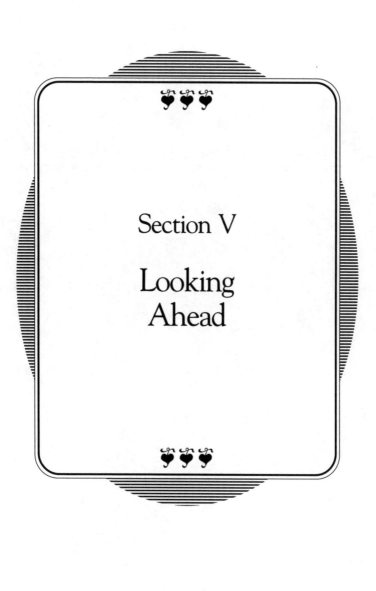

Section V

Looking
Ahead

*F*or I know the plans I have for you" declares the LORD, "plans to prosper you and not to harm you, plans to give you hope and a future."

JEREMIAH 29:11

IN THE FIRST four sections of this book, we've worked our way through the trauma of change—how you can face the reality of it and hold on to hope.

But you know as well as I do that whatever change you've faced, you will someday—maybe quite soon—face even more change. We must acknowledge the fact that as we age, friends move away, some family members and friends will die, our children will leave the nest, and we will eventually retire from our life's occupation. Those changes are quite predictable. But then there are the unpredictable changes—maybe exciting, maybe devastating—that will most certainly come our way.

In the next five chapters we will look ahead to see how God might be preparing you for changes you will face in the future, and what you can do to be ready for the next install-ment of the winds of change in your life.

To do this we will look at the life of Jesus' disciple Peter. Going about his regular duties on a perfectly ordinary day, Peter, a simple, hard-working fisherman, and his brother heard an extraordinary voice say an amazing thing: "Come, follow me . . . and I will make you fishers of men" (Matthew 4:19).

Jesus' summons and Peter's response ushered Peter into a change that revolutionized his own life and in some measure the history of the world. How did God prepare Peter for that day?

Chapter · 21 ·

The Preparation

It is written in Isaiah the prophet:
"I will send my messenger ahead of you,
who will prepare your way"—
"a voice of one calling in the desert,
'Prepare the way for the Lord,
make straight paths for him.' "
And so John came . . .

Mark 1:2–4a

STANDING ON THE banks of the Jordan River, John the Baptist cried out, "Prepare the way for the Lord." Repent. Turn to God.

We don't know for sure that Peter physically heard the voice of John the Baptist. But he surely knew the words of Isaiah and likely had heard of John's unusual presentation; John was like an old-fashioned prophet boldly speaking out the Word of God to a wayward generation.

We have every indication that Peter was a devout man who had turned to God and heeded John's call to repentance. Peter was in one sense prepared for the coming of the Lord, looking for the Messiah, the King, to come and put His kingdom in place. But he had no way of knowing that preparing the *way* meant preparing a *heart*.

And could Peter have possibly known just how close at hand the Messiah was—walking toward him on the beach one ordinary morning? He couldn't have known how far the encounter would lead or what it would cost.

Yet isn't it interesting that he immediately left his nets, his business, his routine, when he heard that voice? Could he have thought he was responding to a brief conversation or an invitation to a one-day seminar? Did he leave his nets so easily because he thought he would be returning shortly to finish his day's work?

You see, he may have been prepared to follow Jesus, but he certainly wasn't ready. If he had expected a dramatic, permanent change to come about that day, wouldn't he have sold his boat, his nets—his business?

Some changes we can thoroughly prepare for. We paint our houses and get them ready to sell. We read the employment section of the paper looking for a better job, even while we work at the secure one we have. We take classes and fit them into our already busy schedules—preparing for a possible change of career.

But what about the day we get a call from school that our child has been seriously injured? And what about the unexpected pregnancy? The automobile accident? Or the sudden resignation of a beloved pastor? All of these things have happened to me. Yet, while I was caught less than ready, I was not unprepared. Let me explain.

There is a difference between being taken by surprise and being unprepared. Many things take us by surprise, but, as Christians living in God's love and drawing strength from daily doses of His Word, we are constantly being prepared.

Can you think of a time in your own experience when you were taken by surprise, but, because you were prepared, you were able to navigate the difficulty successfully and even grow stronger because of it?

If you face change in the future and become overwhelmed with the feeling that you have been caught off guard, remember this: God wasn't. You might be surprised by the changes that challenge you next week, but God isn't.

When Jesus called Peter, He knew Peter wouldn't return

to his full-time small business as a fisherman in partnership with his brother; yes, He knew even if Peter didn't. And whatever change God is asking you to make right now or in the future, He knows the subsequent ripple-effect changes that will be required, even if you don't.

Furthermore, even if change comes by surprise, you can be prepared. The message of John the Baptist still holds for us today: "Prepare the way of the Lord." The directive is still effective: Turn to God.

In the changes you are facing at the moment, do you feel

_____ unprepared,
_____ taken off guard,
_____ surprised?

Looking back, is there anything that could possibly have warned or stirred you for these changes? Even if you are surprised by change in the near future, what can you do that will help you to prepare for it?

Chapter
· 22 ·

The Proposition

As Jesus was walking beside the Sea of Galilee, he saw two brothers, Simon called Peter and his brother Andrew. They were casting a net into the lake, for they were fishermen. "Come, follow me," Jesus said, "and I will make you fishers of men." At once they left their nets and followed him.

Matthew 4:18–20

"COME. FOLLOW ME."

No introductions. No opening lines. No sales gimmicks—just a simple invitation that would mark the change in Peter's life forever.

Step from the boat, Jesus was saying. Peter had made this simple move every day when the fishing was done, but today it was different. Today he would step from the boat—never to return to lake fishing as the center of his life.

Lay down your net. Another day, Peter would have thrown the net across the water and gathered it in again—full of fish, maybe not so full.

But today he made the move toward becoming someone quite different—a fisher of men.

How did he make the dramatic change? By first leaving

his nets—the familiar, that which he knew best—and then following Christ.

Christ comes to each of us with the same invitation. *Come, leave the familiar, the dependable, the secure. Follow Me. Set aside your own hopes and dreams and embrace Mine. Leave your nets in the water; you won't need them anymore. You are in for a change.*

Think what it would be like to leave whatever you are currently busy with, whatever keeps you tied to the shore, so to speak, and with full trust and abandon follow Christ wherever He would lead. If He came along today and spoke those words to you, "Follow Me," would you have to give a two-weeks' notice or sell the business? Would you have to fix up the house, put it on the market, and wait for a buyer?

He's still saying it—"Come. Follow Me." We just have to listen, and be prepared.

It is interesting to note that Peter didn't leave fishing forever. Other scenes from the Gospels show him at his old task. But in the sense of leaving it as the sole occupation of his life, he did leave it. He may have thrown the same net into the same spot in the lake, but after Jesus called him, it was only to catch fish for his lunch, not sustain his life.

"Come," Jesus says to you and me today. "Follow Me." We may not understand where He will lead or when we will return. His call will likely come in the middle of our everyday routines, but it will connect us to His eternal plans and purposes.

———

What everyday activity do you do that you would not want Jesus to interrupt with an invitation to follow Him?

When is it the easiest for you to hear His voice? When is it the most difficult?

When would it be the easiest to "leave your nets" and make a change?

Are you ready? Do you feel you are not fully prepared or qualified? Don't worry, because with the invitation comes a promise. . . .

Chapter
· 23 ·

The Promise

This is the word that came to Jeremiah from the
LORD: *"Go down to the potter's house, and there I will*
give you my message." So I went down to the potter's
house, and I saw him working at the wheel. But the pot
he was shaping from the clay was marred in his hands; so
the potter formed it into another pot, shaping it as seemed
best to him.

Then the word of the LORD *came to me: "O house*
of Israel, can I not do with you as this potter does?"
declares the LORD. *"Like clay in the hand of the potter,*
so are you in my hand, O house of Israel."

Jeremiah 18:1–6

"COME, FOLLOW ME," Jesus said to Peter and his brother
in Matthew 4:19. Then what? *Come along. Stay close to me*
and watch carefully how I work and what I do. Notice whom I
pick out to heal or deliver and take careful notes. Then, when you
think you've got it down, give it a try, and we'll see if you have
what it takes to be My disciple. Is that the proposition Jesus made
to Peter? Of course not.

The invitation—"Come, follow me."—was linked inex-
tricably to a promise: "And I will make you—" What? Fishers
of men—like Christ himself.

The words, "I will make you," turns my thoughts to the Book of Jeremiah, where God describes himself as a Potter-Craftsman lovingly reworking the clay of a marred pot. Using and highlighting the best qualities of that particular piece of clay, He molds it as seems best to Him.

Many times we Christians forget that following Christ means allowing Him to *make* us. Make us into what we were not before, into what He can use to build His kingdom, and to be what He wants us to be.

Many of us are like the aspiring author who refuses to sit down and write. You may want to have a published book in hand, but are you ready to learn, and practice the self-discipline and sacrifice being published requires?

The same could be said of the would-be soul winner, or preacher, or soloist. Do we want the reward without paying the price? Do you want to have it made without going through the process of having Christ make you?

"I will make you," Christ promises. It is the promise of a process. The promise of becoming, not arriving.

Imagine yourself as clay in the hands of the Master Potter. If He is to mold you into the vessel He can best use, you must remain soft, pliable, ready to accept change, ready to be changed.

The alternative? Being resistant can cause the inevitable change to toughen and harden our hearts. If we see an imperfection or scar in ourselves, we tend to hide it, protect it, even from our loving Maker and Redeemer. But nothing is hidden from Him. If we open ourselves to God, He can and will rework our flaws into marks of beauty. He wants to fashion us into His image, His own likeness.

The promise made to Peter is offered to you today. Do you hear Christ saying, "Come, follow me. Let me make you. Like clay in the hand of the potter, so are you in my hand"?

May your response be that of Isaiah the prophet: "Yet, O LORD, you are our Father. We are the clay, you are the potter; we are all the work of your hand" (Isaiah 64:8). To paraphrase: "Work away, Lord. Make me."

———

What have you been hiding or protecting from being touched by the Lord?

If He were to reshape you, what would you have to let Him remold?

_____ past hurts
_____ disappointments
_____ resentment
_____ mistrust
_____ hopelessness
_____ self-righteousness
_____ independence
_____ doubt
_____ other:

How does the promise of God's making or remaking you help you to hold on to hope?

Chapter · 24 ·

God's Provision

Immediately Jesus made the disciples get into the boat and go on ahead of him to the other side, while he dismissed the crowd. After he had dismissed them, he went up on a mountainside by himself to pray. When evening came, he was there alone, but the boat was already a considerable distance from land, buffeted by the waves because the wind was against it.

During the fourth watch of the night Jesus went out to them, walking on the lake. When the disciples saw him walking on the lake, they were terrified. "It's a ghost," they said, and cried out in fear.

But Jesus immediately said to them: "Take courage! It is I. Don't be afraid."

"Lord, if it's you," Peter replied, "tell me to come to you on the water."

"Come," he said.

Then Peter got down out of the boat, walked on the water and came toward Jesus. But when he saw the wind, he was afraid and, beginning to sink, cried out, "Lord, save me!"

Immediately Jesus reached out his hand and caught him. "You of little faith," he said, "why did you doubt?"

And when they climbed into the boat, the wind died down. Then those who were in the boat worshiped him, saying, "Truly you are the Son of God."

Matthew 14:22–32

SNOOPY WANTS TO be a writer. He gets out his old manual typewriter and begins every attempt, "It was a dark and stormy night. . . ." But then his inspiration dies. Snoopy needs to interview Peter.

Peter lived through an unforgettable dark and stormy night. Who could forget such an experience?

In the middle of a raging storm, he saw and finally recognized Jesus coming toward him. He was not in a big, secure, Coast Guard patrol boat, but he was walking. Walking in the middle of the lake, on top of the very waves that were threatening to capsize the fishing boat that Peter and the others were bailing water from.

"Come," Jesus said. "Leave the boat." Familiar words to Peter. Jesus had spoken them before. But that was on a calm day. It's one thing to leave a boat that is pulled safely to shore. You can step out onto the beach and walk on the pebbles with the Lord. But leave the boat, here? Now? And walk where?

The first time Jesus invited Peter to leave the boat, He was asking Peter to take a giant step. But this invitation was to take an impossible leap. If the inviting voice was from God, it was material for a miracle. But if it weren't? If seeing Jesus were only a vision that Peter had invented in his mind, stepping out would be a plunge into disaster.

What a choice! What a challenge! Maybe not so unlike the choices and challenges you and I face from time to time.

Some of the changes you face in the future will be fierce storms. Your "boats" of security will be buffeted and seem ready to capsize. But wait. Off in the distance appears a lone figure coming toward you. It is Jesus. You may not recognize Him at first. He may appear in a way you don't expect and do things you haven't seen Him do before.

But if you listen, you can hear Him speak above the noise

128

of the storm. Words of comfort and courage: "It is I. Don't be afraid."

Seeing Jesus in the distance, even hearing His comforting words, may not be enough. You may have to close the gap between you. Though hearing His voice is a comfort, you need to be closer to Him.

"Jesus!" you cry.

"Come," He says. "Get out of the boat."

Get out of the boat? Is He serious?

Yes, there are times when you—when I—need to get out of the boat. We may even be forced out of the boat. And we can "walk on water"—if we keep our eyes fastened securely on Him and not on the wind whipping around us.

But, you might say, Peter was in Jesus' physical presence. How do we—here and now—catch sight of Him and catch His hand?

What Peter did by sight, we must do in faith.

Faith, the *substance* of things hoped for. Faith, the *evidence* of things not seen (Hebrews 11:1, KJV).

Through focusing on the promises of God's Word, we are able to step away from our "boats" of security. Not in presumption or irresponsibly, but at His invitation. "Come," He is saying to us. And with that invitation He also gives the following promises of provision:

2 Corinthians 9:8: "And God is able to make all grace abound to you, so that in all things at all times, having all that you need, you will abound in every good work."

Ephesians 3:20: "Now to him who is able to do immeasurably more than all we ask or imagine, according to his power that is at work within us . . ."

Philippians 4:19: "And my God will meet all your needs according to his glorious riches in Christ Jesus."

If you write these promises on cards and post them where you can frequently see them, they will remind and encourage you. But stamp them indelibly on your heart, and they will change you.

Next time you read the Sunday comics and good ol' Snoopy is at his manual typewriter, making yet another attempt at his book, think of your own dark and stormy nights. Think of the promises God has made and kept to you as you have had the courage to leave the boat—your security—to step out to get close enough to the Lord to catch His hand.

Next time you need courage and faith to step out, remember God's faithfulness in the past—to Peter, and to you.

Next time Snoopy needs inspiration, maybe he should skip his interview with Peter and interview you!

In Matthew 14:31 Jesus asked Peter, "Why did you doubt?" Try to identify what made Peter doubt. (He already had been walking on the water!) When you begin to doubt, what typically sets your doubt in motion?

———————

Next time, what can you do to turn your back on doubt?

Choose one verse of scripture that will help you to fix your eyes on Christ in the midst of the next storm. Memorize that verse today.

Chapter
· 25 ·

Follow Me

When Peter saw [John], he asked, "Lord, what about
him?" Jesus answered, ". . . what is that to you? You
must follow me."

John 21:21–22*

"I'M GOING FISHING," one of the disciples said to his six
friends.

"Okay, we'll go with you," another said, and all seven
entered their boat and set out to sea late in the evening on
the darkening waters.

In the last few days, nothing had been the same. Before
the crucifixion, the twelve had been inseparable. Since then,
they had not held together very well. Jesus had appeared to
them on at least two occasions—but they still felt direction-
less, like a boat drifting. Maybe life would never be the same
again.

At least one of these men, Peter, had to live with his
cowardly betrayal of Christ. If only Jesus had brought it up
when he appeared to them! At least Peter would know where
he stood. Now he returned to the familiarity of fishing—at
least he knew what to expect from the boat and the sea.

---

*You may wish to read all of John 21 for full impact and benefit.

There on the sea, Peter could stare out into the night and face his black mood. The water beneath the small craft bobbed and shifted, up and down, like his own fluctuating emotions. Occasionally, the salty sea water sprayed a bitterness onto his lips, dampening his hair and clothes—cold as his regret. Again and again, they pulled up the heavy nets. Empty. Empty. Empty.

Toward morning, Peter ached—bone and muscle. The night's labor failed to produce anything. It all spoke to Peter of his own depressing future. The predawn fog turned to a light morning mist, and by the now-streaming daylight, the mist rolled toward the water's edge. From the corner of his eye, Peter caught sight of the lone figure, standing near a campfire on the beach. Then, the voice . . .

"Friends! How is the fishing?"

Someone called back, "Not so good."

"Try the other side of the boat."

"What did he say?" the fishermen asked each other.

"I think he said try the other side."

"Right," grumbled Peter.

"What have we got to lose?"

One more cast—and the net was overloaded! Too heavy for the small boat to carry. John straightened his back and looked toward the Man who was patiently waiting on shore. "It is the Lord!"

In a moment, Peter dove from the boat . . . leaving the fishing business behind for good.

Jesus would ask Peter, within the hearing of all his friends, "Do you love me?"

"Of course, I do. You know my heart, you know I love you," said Peter.

"Then feed my sheep," said Jesus—not once, but three times.

Can it be? Is there something I can do after all? thought Peter.

Three times Peter denied Christ, three times Christ recommissioned him. Peter's would not be a life adrift in uncertainty. The Lord would not leave him anchored on a mistake. His life was to have meaning, a destination—not only for himself, but for others.

Of course, Peter's humanity remained intact.

"But what about him?" Peter wanted to know, nodding in John's direction. There had been strange talk about John.

"What I do with him, in him, or for him is none of your business," Jesus said in effect. "Your business—no matter what it costs you—is to follow Me."

What about you? Think about the changes that have come to your life and the decisions you have made. Maybe they have turned out all right, maybe not. No matter. Today you can hear Christ saying to you as He said to Peter, "I still have a plan for your life. It is still this: *Follow Me.*"

Peter would live a life that glorified God. You and I are called to do the same.

Can you hear the voice of your Savior calling, "Follow Me"? Today, listen to the voice and hear the call again—perhaps for the very first time.

Recall the time when you first decided to follow Christ. What has come into your life that has gotten you off track from His simple summons?

If you were to simply follow Christ, no matter what other people did, how would you need to change?

What is your answer to His call—"Follow Me"?

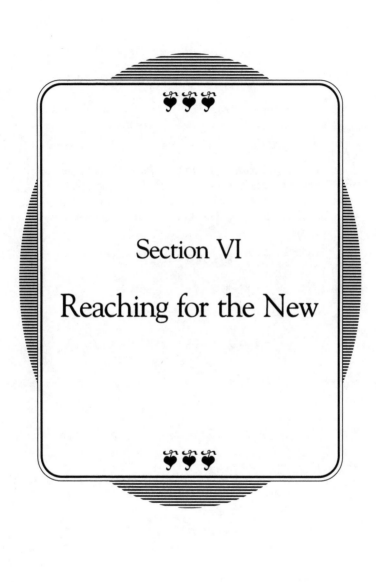

Section VI

Reaching for the New

Y ou were taught, with regard to your former way of life, to put off your old self, which is being corrupted by its deceitful desires; to be made new in the attitude of your minds; and to put on the new self, created to be like God in true righteousness and holiness.

EPHESIANS 4:22–24

"AT THIS POINT IN TIME"—inflated phrase perfectly describes where you are right now. This very moment, this precise instant is the point in time separating your past from your future, your yesterday from your tomorrow. There's truth in the old cliché: Today is the first day of the rest of your life. This exact point in time is the moment you must seize to make positive change. This moment offers opportunity for newness.

The next five chapters will help you explore the possibilities for the new. What does God have in mind for your tomorrows?

Chapter
· 26 ·

Looking
for Change

"*The time is coming, declares the Lord,*
when I will make a new covenant
with the house of Israel
and with the house of Judah.
It will not be like the covenant
I made with their forefathers. . . .
This is the covenant I will make with the house of Israel
after that time, declares the Lord.
I will put my laws in their minds
and write them on their hearts.
I will be their God,
and they will be my people. . . ."
By calling this covenant *"new,"* he has made the first
one obsolete; and what is obsolete and aging will soon
disappear.

Hebrews 8:8–10, 13

HOW MANY TIMES have you said to yourself, *There's got
to be a better way?* If you're like most people, you've probably
not only said it, you've actually looked for and found a better
way to do certain things.

Entire industries have been built—or rebuilt—and maintained long and profitable lives because they have asked that question and challenged their employees with it. Here's why: Looking for a better way keeps design engineers motivated and inventors creating and, in turn, keeps manufacturers on the leading, competitive edge. Looking for a better way is good for people, and it's good for business.

I remember Mama smiling, even chuckling, as she did laundry every Monday in a wringer washer. She was remembering that her mother had scrubbed her wash on a washboard. But now Monday is not necessarily washday in my house, because I can run a load in my automatic whenever I choose—on the way out the door, before I go to bed, or when I get home from the office. Not only is my laundry chore physically easier; my Mondays have been virtually freed up to use another way.

My husband fondly remembers his 1957 Chevy. It was yellow and white, sleek and wonderfully heavy. But by today's standards? It weighed a ton, had no air conditioning, and was a gas guzzler.

A few years back I wrote my first book in a spiral notebook, with a ballpoint pen. Soon I found it easier to write with a Smith-Corona manual typewriter. Then I moved up to a used electric one. Within ten years I was sitting at a computer, moving around whole paragraphs at the push of a key. In the few years since I first touched a computer keyboard, I have upgraded my system's software and have learned desk-top publishing.

Each of these changes has been because someone asked the question: Isn't there a better way?

Maybe you have struggled with your walk toward maturity—becoming the kind of Christian you want to become. You have stubborn attitudes and habits that refuse to give way, even to the most rigid determination and discipline. Maybe you have old hurts and wounds that hang on despite repetitious rituals of forgiveness and decisions to forget and go on.

Some give in to the temptation to keep the hurt and the destructive habits as a way of life, accepting the misbelief, *This is just the way I am; this is life.*

But think about it. Would a God who knew that the law could not save anyone, who gave His only Son to die to fulfill the law no one could keep, would this loving, totally selfless God stop short and leave you or me in misery—powerless—for the rest of our lives?

Of course not. His unchangeable, undeniable Word confirms it. There is a better way. His name is Jesus. He is the Way. He is your way to the change for the better you need.

Jesus, the only Way, the better Way, makes all other ways and methods of trying to improve ourselves obsolete. His way opens up a whole new world of hope and possibilities. He makes it possible for us to make a radical departure from our past and look with new eyes upon our future, all the while adding a new dimension to our todays.

Yes, some things do have to change. We need to change. And we need a way to do it. Jesus is the way. He provides unrestricted access to the Father for us. He will not mislead you or victimize you. He will show you a clear and untainted pathway to peace with God.

How do you walk in His way? Whenever you are faced with a problem, a question, or are struggling, turn to Him. Quietly, humbly, speak His name. Jesus has the power to break through the strongholds that bind you. His power cuts through any red tape you have conceived or perceived that keeps you from your heavenly Father. That name, when barely whispered, breaks through the barriers of time and space and reverberates through the chambers of heaven until it falls on God's ears.

Now during this time of change and adjustment, call upon Jesus. Let the Good Shepherd love you, let Him lead you. Let Him change you.

What areas of your life, especially attitudes or habits, do you feel need to be changed?

In what personal relationships have you said, "There must be a better way"?

Write a letter to Jesus and ask for His help.

Date:

Dear Jesus,

Chapter
· 27 ·

When Only
New
Will Do

"I will give them an undivided heart and put a new spirit
in them; I will remove from them their heart of stone and
give them a heart of flesh."

Ezekiel 11:19

Sing to the LORD a new song,
For he has done marvelous things.

Psalm 98:1

EVERY EASTER of my childhood we made the trek into town
to attend church with our relatives. We left behind the desert
for a brief overnight visit where there were lawns and sidewalks.

Along with hidden Easter baskets and a new dress, I always
had new shoes. Shoes of patent leather or white "Mary Janes"
with straps and sometimes little holes punched in delicate
patterns. One time I wore red ones with straps and two buck-
les. Wonderful, new shoes!

Much too early in the morning, I would get myself as ready
as I could—new dress, new shoes—and walk up and down on
the sidewalk in front of Aunt Peggy's house. I loved the way
those new shoes made magic crackling sounds as I walked

under the pepper trees, stepping on the little seeds that had fallen to the cement.

New shoes, sidewalks, and little popping seeds. Nothing could please me more. Old shoes didn't make quite the same sound or have the same feel as those new ones. Yes, there are times when only new will do.

When my daughters married, there were some old familiar things that went with them into their new lives. But in some cases only new would do—a new wedding dress and lingerie, of course, and then new towels, sheets, blankets, new dishes, pots and pans.

God offers His people "new"—because only new will do.

In Ephesians 4:22–23 we are told "to put off your old self . . . and to put on the new self, created to be like God in true righteousness and holiness." (See also Colossians 3.) Only a new self will do. New attitudes, a new outlook, new habits, new motivations, new opportunities, new challenges—all are available because of a renewed mind (Romans 12:2).

"Therefore, if anyone is in Christ, he is a new creation; the old has gone, the new has come!" (2 Corinthians 5:17).

As you reflect on the new thing God is doing in and through you, you quickly see that only a new song of praise will do. The songs of praises you sang yesterday belong to yesterday. Sing unto the Lord a new song—a song for today. Because only a new song of praise will do.

Turn in your Bible to Isaiah 43:19. Highlight or underline the first phrase: "See, I am doing a new thing!" Take your Bible outside, or go to a window where you can "lose yourself" in the view of the sky and God's handiwork. Be absolutely quiet before God. Do not tell God your problems. Rather, let His words from this passage sink deep into you. With every breath you inhale, think: *"See, I am doing a new thing!"* With every breath you exhale, think, *Old things are passing away.*

Let a consciousness of God's closeness surround you. Let the promise of newness become absolute and real. Don't hurry this. Sometimes we get so used to coping with the old, it is difficult to experience the promise of the new.

Later, place two chairs, one at each end of a table. Take two sheets of paper. Label the top of one "old" and the other "new." Place one paper at each end of the table.

On the paper labeled "old" write some of the things you wish God would change or help you change. When that list is finished, walk to the other end of the table, aware with each step of how you are actually moving away from the old, even before the new list is written.

Now write a list of the new things you see God doing or that you are asking Him to do in you.

When you have finished, hold the list marked "old" before the Lord. Ask Him to help you with these things. Then tuck the list away in a safe place, where you can refer to it later, but where others will not find it. Put the "new" list in your Bible and refer to it often. As you read it, sing a new song of praise to God.

Take out the "old" list occasionally to make notes of progress or change. You may wish to add to either list from time to time.

Chapter · 28 ·

A Terrific, Terrifying New Thing

"See, I am doing a new thing!
Now it springs up; do you not perceive it?
I am making a way in the desert
and streams in the wasteland."

Isaiah 43:19

ON A DATE as a teenager, I tentatively stepped into a roller coaster car—second from the front. I sat on the red vinyl-covered seat and took hold of the icy-cold bar that rested loosely across my lap. I wondered if it could really keep me from plunging to my death, then quickly shut the thought from my mind.

With a little jerk, then a mild lurch, the car moved slowly forward. This wasn't too bad, I comforted myself. A gentle dip, a graceful curve, and then the slow, long climb upward until the car was almost to a complete stop. From that perspective I could see for miles.

But before I could even begin to enjoy the scenic view, I felt the bottom fall out, as I was heaved forward over the edge and propelled toward the ground below. Suddenly my head snapped back, pinned to my seat. A full-body scream began in the pit of my stomach, swelled through my chest, and exploded as it burst from my mouth.

This is insane! I want off! The little train accelerated and I had no choice but to go the distance. Hurled to the right, flung to the left. I was tossed and propelled, plunged and hurled. I heard the wind thunder past my ears and felt it whip my hair.

My heart pounded in my chest as I was yanked, tugged, and twisted. My body was forced against my date's, and then his crushed mine against the side of the car. "Hold on!" he shouted. "Here we go again!"

One more short series of merciless dips and ruthlessly sharp curves, and then we shot into the platform area and came to an abrupt halt.

I fought my way out of the car and staggered to the gate. "Want to go again?" my date shouted.

Are you kidding? This is madness. It's suicidal. It's hazardous and intolerable. "Sure! Let's do it again."

Now, in middle age, the Lord sometimes whispers, "I'm doing a new thing." That's when I grab on as tightly as I can and get ready for the ride of my life.

When God does a new thing in my life, it is unlike any other He has ever done before. It is a thrill, an adventure, and sometimes it scares me to death. But like the roller coaster ride, while it may be terrifying, it is always terrifyingly terrific.

God may be doing a new thing in your life too—right now. Wouldn't it be a shame to resist the thrill of it all? We can be so closed in and afraid—so protective and unadventurous that we could actually stand on the platform while others take all the risks and experience all the adventure.

We can choose to stand secure and safe, all the while feeling the vibration of the train pounding on the tracks looping and curving all around us. We might be able to stand close enough to hear whoops of delight coming from others, even feel the swish of wind as the cars speed by. But if we never get in the car and take our seats, we will never experience anything new.

Living for God—God living in us—is an adventure. It

148

takes courage to navigate the curves and dips and climbs and plunges. But it is outrageously wonderful. And it's always adventurous. Shall we go again?

What terrifying, new thing is stretching out before you? Using the analogy of a roller coaster ride, where are you in relation to a change or changes in your life:

_____ contemplating buying a ticket?

_____ waiting on the platform?

_____ just stepping into the car?

_____ finding a good place to hang on?

_____ beginning the long climb?

_____ at the top of the first hill?

_____ facing an uncertain drop?

_____ plunging down an unending drop?

_____ roaring around a curve?

_____ being shaken by a series of up-and-down dips?

_____ whipping wildly from side to side?

_____ nearing the platform to get off?

_____ staggering to the gate?

_____ getting ready to go again?

If God were to do a radical new thing in your life, how would you most likely perceive yourself? As being pulled, flung, and battered, or stretched, shaped, and molded? Give reasons why.

What potential for change do you see after you have experienced a major new direction in your life?

Chapter
· 29 ·

❧
Mercy—
Manna
for the Soul
❧

Because of the LORD'S great love we are not consumed,
for his compassions never fail. They are new every
morning; great is your faithfulness.

Lamentations 3:22–23

DAY AFTER DAY, the routine was the same. The tent-wife
of Israel in the wilderness started her chores with the gathering
of the morning manna. Just an "omer" for each person in her
family. Then she went home to prepare it in one of two ways—
baked like biscuits, or boiled like dumplings. The same food
every day. (See Exodus 16.)

In our day of choice and variety, such a limited menu
would fast become dull and boring. Can't you see our children
coming in for breakfast, looking in their cereal bowls and
saying in their most disgusted tone, "Gross! Manna again!"

Monotonous as it sounds, manna provides a delightful picture—an illustration of God's mercy.

Mercy and manna are much alike—both fall new every
morning. But because it falls fresh, it can't be stored for another time.

As the children of Israel could depend on manna, we can
depend on God's mercy when we are also stuck in the middle

151

of life's deserts. Just when we think we will die in our wilderness experiences, God miraculously feeds our hungry spirits and refreshes our weary souls. He reaches out to us with His love and compassion that is new in deeper dimensions every day.

If your day offers you hopelessness, God offers love and mercy. If you are facing the challenge of new opportunities or the sorrow of loss, God's mercy never fails. Whether your heart is soaring with the excitement of a new love or with the tragedy of rejection and betrayal—God's faithfulness is great.

But there is a danger for us in the "mercy/manna diet." Like manna, mercy can be taken for granted. On the first morning that the manna flakes fell, it must have been exciting to the hungry people. Nothing was more delicious. But after thirty days, with no variation. . . . How many times do I—do you—take for granted God's mercy?

One of the dangers of the Christian's life is that after many months or years, the stone-solid dependability of God's love can become routine. Like the Israelite tent-wife gathering manna, our daily quiet time can become simply routine: We habitually read the Bible, with no thought of gathering mercy/manna for the day; we do what we think we "should" instead of waking every day aware of our need and the newness of His mercy toward us. If we're not careful our devotional life can become like a daily chore—a dead and obligatory discipline—instead of a moment in the light and presence of the Master.

Have you lost your joy—your wonder: *God makes available to mere human beings His mercy! God pours out His love to us!*

Every day, gather what you need. Depend on more to be there when you need it tomorrow. And guard your heart from taking a careless attitude toward His mercy—the manna for our souls.

This is the miracle: God's mercy is not just *there* every morning—but *new* every morning. Make it a practice to live with a heart-attitude of appreciation and thankfulness.

———

What's the difference between taking God's mercy for granted and depending on it?

Have you taken His love and His Word for granted? In what ways?

What are some of the ways in which you can restore the freshness of His manna for your soul?

"I should read the Bible more; pray more; love more; give more." Sound familiar? What are some words that would speak of a fresh, new attitude toward God and His faithfulness toward us?

Chapter
· 30 ·

Persevere for
a Purpose

*Consider it pure joy, my brothers, whenever you face
trials of many kinds, because you know that the testing of
your faith develops perseverance. Perseverance must
finish its work so that you may be mature and complete,
not lacking anything.*

James 1:2–4

*But the seed on good soil stands for those with a noble
and good heart, who hear the word, retain it, and by
persevering produce a crop.*

Luke 8:15

IN THIS STUDY we've talked a lot about transitions, about
hope, about holding on. We've talked about letting go of the
old and reaching out to the new.

As you walk into God's wonderful, new challenge, remember this short commentary on one of the oldest stories recorded
in the Bible: "You have heard of Job's perseverance and have
seen what the Lord finally brought about" (James 5:11).

As Job persevered, God worked—bringing about the new.

James 1:4 says that perseverance "must finish its work" if
we are to be mature and complete. Are you complete? Totally

mature in your attitudes and conversation? If you are like the rest of us, there is at least *some* progress yet to be made.

It's amazing to me: The older I get, the more I recognize maturity in some areas and see the embarrassing lack of it in others. I also know that the areas in which I can see a measurable growth toward maturity are the very areas in which I have had to persevere the most.

That means persevering through problems. Consider Romans 5:3–5, which links suffering to perseverance and perseverance to character and character to hope, all in the context of rejoicing in the love of God: "We also rejoice in our sufferings, because we know that suffering produces perseverance; perseverance, character; and character, hope. And hope does not disappoint us, because God has poured out his love into our hearts by the Holy Spirit, whom he has given us."

One of my favorite songs of the seventies was the Gaithers' "Through It All." A line of the lyrics raises an interesting scenario: If we never had problems, we wouldn't know that God could solve them. Yes, Jesus meets us in our needs. He helps us solve our problems, and He mends our hurts—but many times He does it while we are persevering.

It even means persevering under pressure. First Corinthians 10:13 says, "No temptation has seized you except what is common to man. And God is faithful; he will not let you be tempted beyond what you can bear. But when you are tempted, he will also provide a way out so that you can stand up under it."

We persevere in obedience. We persevere in forgiveness. We persevere in God's mercy. We persevere in His love and by His grace. We keep plugging away no matter what. Like the little Energizer Battery Bunny, we keep going and going and going . . . because . . .

We persevere toward a promise. "Therefore, since we are surrounded by such a great cloud of witnesses, let us throw off everything that hinders and the sin that so easily entangles, and let us run with perseverance the race marked out for us" (Hebrews 12:1).

And Paul wrote, "Forgetting what is behind and straining toward what is ahead, I press on toward the goal to win the prize for which God has called me heavenward in Christ Jesus."

Since you started this study, how has your outlook toward change been altered?

How has your view of God changed?

Write out a summary of the three most important things you learned in this study.

A Final Challenge

AT FORTY-FOUR, Millie Brown, a single mother who had often worked three jobs to raise her three children alone, decided to train for the "Iron Man"—a triathalon that could defeat even the most able athlete.

It took Millie an entire year before she could jog a mile. Three years later she entered the race requiring a two-and-one-half-mile swim, one-hundred-mile bike ride, and twenty-six-mile run to the finish line. I watched her race on TV, and the effort almost killed Millie. She fell twice during the twenty-six-mile run. Once, she was put on a stretcher and into a waiting ambulance—but before the door was shut she came crawling out! Her goal was to finish the race if it meant crawling every inch of the last few remaining miles.

For Millie, just to *finish* was to win. She wasn't running against anyone else, nor against the clock. She was running against everything in her life that said she was a loser. She was competing against her past, her failures, her lost opportunities and her low self-image. She had to finish . . . just *had* to.

Sitting in front of the TV that day, I began to shout scripture sentiments at the screen.

"Forget what is behind, Millie! Press on!" (Philippians 3:13–14).

"Run the race to which you have been called, Millie!" (Revelation 2:10).

"Keep going, Millie! It's okay if it's hard! Just keep going! There is a reward for you at the finish line!" (James 1:12).

I was riveted to the TV—totally involved with Millie's race. Having never heard of her before that day, I suddenly realized that I needed Millie to finish the course—not for her, but for me!

Finishers do not just finish for their own sakes, but many times are just the example, the role model, that someone else looks to for the motivation to finish themselves—encouraging someone else, in turn.

Whatever you are facing, whatever you have been through, no matter how many times you have fallen during the course of your race, get up—the finish line is ahead. Life is not about coming in first, it's about *coming in*—period!

Other "Iron Man" competitors stood around at the finish line, waiting for Millie. Some even went back to walk, run, or crawl beside her. *Everyone's celebration depended on Millie's crossing the finish line.*

This is a challenge to you and to me—to persevere!—The crown of life is waiting!—I hear there is one sized just for you. . . .

———

Name three people whom you have seen persevere in the face of great odds:

How does watching them persevere help you?

Name three people who would be encouraged to see you persevere:

1.

2.

3.

Write out a new commitment to persevere:

Leader's
Notes

GROUP GUIDELINE SUGGESTIONS

As mentioned at the beginning of this book, if this study is used in a group setting, members should study the five entries of each section throughout the week in preparation for discussion at the weekly meeting. In this way, the material is covered in six weeks. A group may decide to spend more or less time on a given section depending on the needs of the participants. Discussion questions are included at the end of these leader's notes.

A good general group approach to this study is one of personal investigation and shared responses. Discussion questions will help bring out even more insight into application for personal growth.

In the course of covering the material, some very private areas of personal discovery may be exposed or brought to mind. A leader should not expect, nor force, everyone to participate each time or respond to each discussion question. Do encourage even the slightest participation with affirmative comments, regardless of the contribution.

Because this is a responsive study, there are no wrong answers. The nature of the study tends to get to the heart of many emotional issues. Some people in your group may desperately need a listening ear, and a correction from you may discourage them from participating in the discussion, or even keep them from attending your group again. Allow the Holy Spirit to do the correcting and a deep work of patience and sensitivity in you, the leader.

Once in a while, there will be a member of a group who monopolizes the conversation or goes off on a tangent. If so, very carefully approach that person afterward and ask if you can be of help individually. There may be times during the study when a person may genuinely come to a breakthrough, drawing the attention of the group to herself and her needs exclusively. That would be the exception, however, and not the rule.

If someone in your group asks a question, don't take the sole responsibility for having an answer. Allow others in the group to contribute. If you do give an answer, give it after others have spoken.

There are three basic group rules that you should follow without fail:

1. *Start and end on schedule.* Everyone is busy. Set your meeting times and stick to them. One and one half hours generally works well for evening groups. Daytime groups may wish to meet for a little longer. Sunday school groups need to meet within an assigned schedule. Actual study and discussion should take only a portion of the meeting time. Fellowship and sharing prayer requests help develop strong bonds within your group. Make time for that to happen.

2. *Begin and end with prayer.* The opening prayer can be a simple offering by one person asking God's blessing on your time together. You may feel the need in your group to have additional time for prayer concerns or needs of the group. (One effective way to handle this is to have everyone write down the name of the person they are concerned for and a very brief statement about the need on a small piece of paper. The slips are put into a basket and redistributed to the group. Each person then offers a sentence prayer concerning the request they have drawn from the basket.) Closing prayers should be centered around the needs that have arisen related to the study and discussion. Bring the

meeting to a close with your own prayer.
3. *Involve everyone.* Many of the issues covered in this study are of a personal nature. Depending on the amount of abuse and misunderstanding your group members have experienced, some may not be ready to discuss the issues they are dealing with. However, during the fellowship time, the time of praying for others, and the ongoing study, seek to build trust and encourage them to open their hearts and share with the group. Find a way to involve even the most reserved people in a way that is comfortable and safe for them.

Discussion times can be rich and rewarding for everyone—that is, everyone who gets to share and discuss. The size of the group somewhat determines the opportunities for sharing. A group of six members is ideal, but a group as large as ten can work. When the group reaches ten, consider the advantages of dividing into smaller groups of three or four for at least a portion of the sharing and discussion time.

Discussion Questions

Orientation—Introduction

You may find it helpful to have an orientation meeting before you begin a group study of this book. Such a meeting will allow members of the group to have opportunity to look over the book and to prepare for the first discussion and sharing time.

The following questions will help your group members get off to a good start and understand what you expect to accomplish in the study.

1. Many people have difficulty fitting a daily quiet time into their routine. What ways have you tried to do this? What ways have worked for you, and what ways did not work?
2. Everyone experiences change from time to time. What are some of the changes you have made successfully, and what are some of your more unsuccessful attempts at change?
3. When we read a book or embark on a new study, not every illustration or example fits our own particular situation. Yet we might find such an illustration to be helpful in some

way. Why do you think this is true?

4. Read aloud the introduction to each study section. After doing this, what are your expectations concerning this study?

Assignment

Everyone should first read "How to Use This Book" at the beginning of the book. Each day for five days before we meet again, read and respond to each of the devotional studies in Section I, "The Challenge of Change." (Before each meeting, members should read and study the five chapters for the section to be discussed at the next meeting.)

Section I: The Challenge of Change

To begin the first study, read together the introduction to the section. Use the following questions as models or thought-starters for group discussion:

1. How can the analogy of a storm be applied to the changes one experiences?
2. Why is change so difficult?
3. How can taking responsibility in the beginning of a transition be more helpful than waiting until it's over to take responsibility?
4. If your transition was compared to "closet-cleaning," what stage are you in?
5. If you knew without doubt that the change you face was a part of God's plan, that the outcome was guaranteed to be positive, and that His power was available to help—how would that change the way you approach the change?
6. Change is an inevitable part of life. Each person in this group is at some point of change. How does knowing that help you?
7. How can we pray for one another? How can we pray for you?

(Leader: Make a list of names with prayer needs and requests.)

Section II: Confronting Change

Read together the introduction to the section and then discuss the following:

1. When are you the most likely to avoid reality? Face reality?
2. Have you ever felt as if you had an "Esther Experience" (If I perish, I perish)? What gave you the courage to face the threat before you?
3. When you read chapter 9, "Know That Some Things Never Change," what mental images or memories of things that never change surfaced for you? How does hanging on to the unchanging things help when you have to make changes?
4. How does God's changelessness help you?
5. How can we help each other confront our changes in ways that give strength?
6. How have you chosen to build new securities?
7. How are you celebrating the changes you are going through?

Section III: Anchored in the God of Hope

Read together the introduction to the section and then discuss the following:

1. How is hope like an anchor?
2. How have you changed your schedule to keep your DQT (Daily Quiet Time)?
3. How can we keep our focus on Christ instead of on our problems?
4. Why is it sometimes easier to ask someone else to take your needs to God than to go to Him directly?
5. When is it important to seek out prayer and ministry from others? Why is it important?
6. What are you praying for that you need to share with the group for additional prayer support? (Leader: Make a prayer list.)
7. Is there a danger in letting careless "praise-phrases" be-

come a part of our everyday conversation? If not, why not? If so, what is the danger?

8. Do you like to find new creative expressions of praise or do you prefer to use and rely on more generic and accepted ones?
9. Who would be brave enough to share a new praise expression and tell how it came about?
10. How does the analogy of the little girl and Daddy playing "jump" play out in your own experience with God?
11. How does our ability to trust or not to trust our own fathers affect our willingness to trust God?

––––––––––

Section IV: Anchored in a Community of Hope

Read together the introduction to the section and then discuss the following:

1. How is being in this group helping you have hope?
2. When are you most likely to avoid or abandon corporate worship and why?
3. What project have you been a part of that helped you feel as if you belonged?
4. How has a group ever disappointed you?
5. When is it most likely that you would be a straggler?
6. Have you ever shared with someone inappropriately or prematurely? What was the result?
7. Name one person with whom you feel you have a "partnership." What makes it work?
8. In what areas are you most gifted? Are you using those gifts? Why or why not?
9. In what ways have you been tempted to give up hope lately?
10. Which of the ten principles for being anchored in hope are already present and operative in your life? Which one do you most need to develop?

––––––––––

Section V: Looking Ahead

Read together the introduction to the section and then discuss the following:

1. In the past how have you been prepared for change?
2. How is God preparing you now for future change?
3. How/when does God speak to you the most?
4. God is saying, "Come." What does that mean to you?
5. If you were to climb up on the Potter's wheel and say, "Please, Lord, remake me into your vessel," what do you think He would want to work on first?
6. Which of the following three verses helps you step out in faith the most and why? 2 Corinthians 9:8; Ephesians 3:20; Philippians 4:19. (Leader: Read each of the verses aloud from a Bible or have three different people read them.)
7. What is the scariest part of "stepping out of the boat" for you? Explain.
8. What implication does "follow me" have for you at this point in your life?

Section VI: Reaching for the New

Read together the introduction to this section. Then discuss the following:

1. What changes have you already faced successfully?
2. Name one area of life in which you feel you could use a little change?
3. What new thing is terrifying you? Where are you in terms of the roller coaster ride?
4. How can you be a more persevering person?
5. How can we help each other more?
6. What is different about your situation than when we started this study?
7. What is different about you?
8. How has your perception of God changed?
9. What is the most important thing you have learned from this study and how has it made a difference for you?
10. Where do we go from here? (Leader: This is the time to

introduce the next study or announce a little break from group study. If the group has grown too large, this is the time to split into smaller groups before going on to another book or study.)